Keep on,
Keeping on

Betty and Norman in proper dress for the "Old Fashioned Sunday"
festivities at Riverside Baptist Church in North Platte, Nebraska.

ᴵᴼ Lake

Keep on, Keeping on

By
NELLIE SNYDER YOST
AND
BETTY ANN HERRICK

Word Services
Lincoln, Nebraska

Additional copies of this book may be ordered from:
Nellie Snyder Yost
1505 West D Street
North Platte, Nebraska 69101

To my loving husband Norman, who has encouraged and backed me all the way,

and my beloved mother, who has been unstinting in her loyal support and,

my dear friend Nellie Yost. Without her this book would not have been written.

Foreword

I have thoroughly enjoyed my association with Betty in the writing of this book. Her infectious good humor, her ability to see good, even mirth, in the grimmest situations, and her unfailing reliance on God and His goodness, have been an inspiration to me.

I was fascinated by her tales of growing up in Bingham Canyon, that delightful mountain city "seven miles long and forty feet wide." Her struggle to find her way out of the religious confusion of the situation into which she was born, and her triumphant testimony in the end, made a captivating story.

We encountered many difficulties and delays: a long hospitalization for me, a serious illness for Betty, some publishing setbacks, only tightened our bond of friendship and made us the more determined to see our book between covers. When everything was finally in place and the book in production, we felt that it had all been divinely directed and that the outcome was exactly right for us, both as to timing and the opportunity for the successful distribution of this book, the culmination of two years of dedicated effort.

Nellie Snyder Yost,
August 15, 1983

Chapter One

My Arrival

I came to Bingham Canyon about nine o'clock in the evening on April 10, 1932. I was about two weeks early and the family wasn't expecting me; my father was at work in the Apex mine and my grandmother was in her room on the first floor of the Knight Hotel. My mother was in her apartment, two floors above Grandma's room, when her first labor pain struck without warning. As soon as she could catch her breath she went down the stairs to Grandma's room.

"It's the baby," she said, "the baby's coming." Grandma hustled her in to her own big bed, then ran down the street about three blocks to Dr. Frazier's house. The doctor lived in rooms behind his little office; Grandma's knocks and calls aroused no one, which meant the doctor was out on a call, maybe miles away, with no telling when he would be back.

Grandma then retraced her steps to Dr. Ravolte's house. Dr. Ravolte was an Italian, not too long over from his homeland, but Grandma was Italian too, and spoke her native tongue fluently. Back at the hotel the doctor took over and all went well, except that he and my grandmother chattered away all

1

the while—and my mother was furious because she couldn't understand a word they said. I wasn't really puny at four and one-half pounds arrival weight, but I wasn't husky, either. The doctor said I was all right, though, and left me to the care of my mother and grandmother.

Since Grandma, who owned and ran the Knight Hotel, had her hands full taking care of the business, my father sent a messenger the next day to my other grandmother on the farm, some twenty-five miles south of Bingham Canyon, asking her to come in and help look after me. Grandma Beckstead arrived the following day. Doctor Frazier had gotten back to town that day, too, and had dropped into the hotel to have a look at me. He said I was fine and turned his attention to Mom. He was talking to her when Grandma Beckstead hurried in.

She went straight to my bassenette to look at me—and screamed, "This baby's dead. She's not breathing." Then she screamed at the doctor, "Pick her up and spank her, spank her hard." The doctor did as she ordered and I coughed up the phlegm that had stopped my breathing. From then on I was a goer.

My father, R. J. Contratto, was Italian. His parents, Matt and Annie, had come over from Italy with their parents and the two families had settled in Rock Springs, Wyoming, where the children grew up. Annie was nineteen and Matt was twenty when they married, after a proper two years' long courtship. Soon afterward they moved to Bingham Canyon, then a hustling new mining town in western Utah. There Grandfather, who had quite a bit of money, built the Knight Hotel.

Grandma ran the hotel and Grandpa went to work in the copper mine at the top of the mountain. They had five sons before Grandpa contracted miner's consumption and died at the age of forty, leaving Grandma to run the hotel and raise the boys. My father, called "Bunny" from his childhood up and the eldest of the five, grew up in Bingham Canyon where he went to school and was a star player on his high school football team. As soon as he was old enough he, too, went to work in the copper mine, "the richest hole on earth."

My mother grew up on the farm where her mother still lived. Her parents were Mormon settlers and she was one of twelve children, most of them younger than herself. She married and had a little boy, Don, then lost her husband. After she married my father they moved into the apartment in the Knight Hotel, where they lived until I was born. My parents were both dark and very good looking; in fact, I believe they were one of the handsomest couples I ever knew.

By the time I came along Grandma Contratto was married again, to one of the men who lived at the hotel and worked in the mine. A big Irishman by the name of Jack Lennon, he had come to America from Ireland when he was nineteen and eventually landed in Bingham Canyon. Handy at doing and fixing all kinds of things, he had made himself so useful to Grandma after she was widowed that she first hired him to help her keep things running at the hotel and then married him.

Grandad Lennon was very special to me. Along with Mom and Dad and Grandma, he was among the first people I can remember. He was a big man, tall and dark and, to me at least, a fine looking fellow. He wore glasses and smoked a pipe and sometimes drank too much, but he was awfully good to me and always let me have my own way. I sat on his lap a lot when I was very little and he'd let me take turns puffing on his pipe with him.

The hotel had eleven rooms on the second floor and eight apartments upstairs on the third. Three or four of the second floor rooms were reserved for the traveling public, people who stayed only a night or two and went on; the rest were rented, on a more or less permanent basis, to single men who worked in the mine. Married people who lived and worked in town, or the mine, stayed in the third floor apartments.

I was the only baby in the hotel at the time and most of the hotel customers made quite a fuss over me. Two of the regular roomers, Frank and Cal, especially liked to play with me, Mom told me later, and often asked to take me to their room where they gave me candy and entertained me. One day they kept me a little too long and I needed to go to the bathroom. I tried to tell them but they didn't understand baby talk for that necessity, so I went ahead and opened their closet door, thinking it was their bathroom. I couldn't see anything in there to use—

except for Frank's new shoes, so I wee-weed in one of them. Mom said he was a good sport about it, but after that they were careful to return me to Mom before another accident happened.

I was a little past two years old when my sister Dottie was born. She was dark, plump, and cute. I had had the center of attention until she came along and, as she grew older and everybody paid more attention to her, I began to get very jealous. Her coal black curly hair was one of her greatest attractions and I decided to even things up a bit—I took the scissors and haggled off her bangs and her long side curls. That was probably the beginning of all the times I was in trouble.

Some of the town's many hotels, including Grandma's, kept call girls. Grandma had two. I can barely remember them as she sold the hotel to the Kennecott Company before I was four and moved to Salt Lake City. My parents then took over the management of the hotel and let the girls go. But I remember that the girls were pretty and very good to me, especially the one called Jean. She used to invite me up to her room on the second floor, where she gave me pretty things and made a fuss over me.

I well remember a lovely dress that Jean gave me shortly before she left Binham Canyon. It had blue butterflies on a white background and a sparkly butterfly pin at the neck. I wanted to wear it all the time but Mom didn't have time to wash it every day and I wouldn't wear it when it was dirty. So it was in the wash every Monday and I wore it every Tuesday until it wore out—or I grew out of it, whichever came first.

While Grandma was still running the hotel I can remember going into the living room on pay day evenings to sit with Grandma and Mom while they visited with some of the roomers who worked in the mine. They were all drinking from pretty glasses and the men held me on their laps and talked to me and laughed at everything I said, until Mom sent me off to bed.

Years later Mom told me that she and Grandma were drinking tea all that time, tea that Grandma had put in a whiskey bottle, and every time the men ordered a round of drinks she poured tea in her glass and Mom's and got fifty cents a glass for it, the same as for the whiskey the men drank. The visiting sometimes went on for hours, Mom said, and she and Grandma got awfully tired of tea.

Those were prohibition times,* and Bingham Canyon was full of stills. Little as I was I knew about them, as did nearly everyone else in town, and one of them was in one of Grandma's third floor apartments. She operated the still and, every so often, had a batch of home brew ready to take off. At those times she sent Grandpa Lennon upstairs to bottle the beer. Grandpa always went up alone, always stayed a long time, and always came down quite drunk.

Grandpa and some of his friends also bought bootleg whiskey by the truck load in Kemmerer, Wyoming, and ran it into Bingham Canyon where they made plenty of money selling it. Grandpa's visible sign of success from that enterprise was the big Lincoln car he bought every spring for as long as he lived in Bingham Canyon. Their business was simply an established way of life in our town, for the miners had to have their beer and whiskey.

I missed Grandma and Grandpa terribly after they moved to Salt Lake, even though I still had plenty to do in Bingham Canyon. By the time I started to school I had explored the town from end to end and knew everybody in it. After Mom took over the management of the hotel we moved downstairs into Grandma and Grandpa's rooms and Mom opened up the dining room to feed the single miners and the transients who stayed at the hotel. The boarders ate first, then the family.

Dad still worked in the mine for awhile after this, and then was employed as the town's chief of police, a job that took more of his time than the mine work had. Taking care of the rooms and apartments, overseeing the kitchen and serving three meals a day to the boarders and her family kept Mom awfully busy, so I was free to do about as I pleased.

---

* Since Betty was only a year old when the Volstead Act, or "prohibition," was repealed, she probably remembers these things only from hearing her folks tell of them.

Naturally curious and never having "met a stranger" in my life, I was on the go and busy all day long. I was a little thing and, though not plump and dimpled like Dottie, people used to "take" to me; I had good friends all over town and said "Hi" and waved to everyone I met on the street and in the stores and restaurants.

Barb and Riley were two of my oldest and best friends. I don't remember their last names, but they lived in one of our third floor apartments and ran a restaurant farther down the street. A short, stocky couple, they loved children and had none of their own. I don't remember the name of the restaurant either; I just called it "Riley's" and spent a good deal of my time there.

Riley's place was located behind a bar run by one of the Greek townsmen. The customers had to go through the bar to get to the restaurant, where Riley was the cook and Barb the waitress. I was a regular visitor, marching through the bar and into the dining room with my "Hi, Barbie," and gobbling up the goodies she always had for me.

Nick the Greek was another of my best friends. A small, dark man, Nick was the town tailor and had his little shop halfway up, or down, the street. I called on him often, popping through his front door into the shop where he had his sewing machine, his long pressing board and his big tailor's iron. A friendly little man, he always seemed glad to see me. I'd visit a little while before I asked him if he was "about to have some coffee." Then he'd take me into his small back room, plug in a little hot plate, put some things in a pan and brew up some Greek coffee.

Nick poured the coffee into two tiny cups and we took it back into the front room, where we sat down and drank it. I felt very grownup, sitting there drinking coffee with Nick the Greek, although I could hardly bear the taste of the thick, bitter-sweet brew—and we didn't drink it, we spooned it out of the little cups. But I liked so much to visit with Nick that I downed the foul stuff anyway and pretended that I liked it.

One of the town's barbers, Mr. Goris, was another Greek, the father of twelve children. I liked that whole family, too, and some of the children, those around my own age, were among my best friends.

But the friend I loved best of all was Big Helen. From the time I was old enough to trot around town by myself I had been going to Big Helen's place, just down the street from the hotel, on the far side of Nick's shop. Big Helen always welcomed me with smiles and loving hugs. A big, bosomy woman, she wore glasses and had straight bobbed hair. She had no teeth, or didn't wear them if she did, and her dresses were old and plain. She wasn't at all attractive but I loved her so much I didn't pay any attention to the way she looked. I didn't know, of course, that Big Helen was a Madam, and that her place, "520 Main," or just "the 520," was the local house of prostitution. And if I had it wouldn't have made any difference. She was just dear Big Helen to me.

During those happy days when I was on the town I was no doubt often a pest, popping in and out of so many places, but the people were always kind and pleasant, visiting with me and giving me candy and other treats. That aspect of my life surely paid off well. Then there was Aunt Ruby and her boy friend. Aunt Ruby was one of Mom's younger sisters who stayed with us one summer and helped out at the hotel. She soon had a boy friend who regularly came courting. They sat in the family parlor and the rest of the Contrattos considerately left them alone, except for me. I joined them and curled up in a big chair to observe. After a little small talk the young man, Bob, would offer me a nickel or a dime to go buy an ice cream cone. I'd clutch the money and run all the way to the Number One drug store, buy the treat and run back to the parlor to eat it.

I lost hardly any observation time, that way, and Bob soon had to offer me another bribe to obtain a bit more privacy. It was a losing proposition for him—except for the occasions when I ran into a friend or playmate who offered superior diversion. If that happened I might not get back to my post in the parlor all evening. In spite of my interference Bob married Aunt Ruby.

I was also very good at hitching rides. We had two taxi drivers in Bingham Canyon. One, Louie Panos, a Greek, was very thin and didn't have much hair. A very neat person, he was friendly and a great storyteller. He had lived in Bingham Canyon almost ever since it started up as a town and could tell the wildest stories about old times in the place and everybody liked to hear him tell about the old days.

The other taxi driver, Frank, was a Basque and quite a bit younger than Louie. He always wore brown suits and a crew haircut. Louie drove a Cadillac and Frank a small car of some kind, but they were both my friends and whenever I was out on the street and one of them came along, going my way, I asked for a ride. The Canyon street was long and steep and I saw no reason why, if they were going my direction anyway, they shouldn't give me a lift for free.

I was a nuisance to my mother too, because, as far back as I can remember, I couldn't abide being dirty. If I even smudged my face or hands a little I had to take a bath and put on all clean clothes. Before long I was taking a bath and changing clothes three times a day and Mom had to do something about it. She used to say I was like a frog in a pool, the way I jumped in and out of the bathtub all day.

Before the days of automatic washers and permanent press fabrics, laundering and ironing so many outfits for me meant so much extra work for my busy mother that she took to keeping a sharp eye on me and heading me off from the bathtub as often as she could.

Another thing I couldn't abide was staying away from home overnight. Even today I still want to be in my own bed when night comes, and when I was a child I'd do almost anything to make sure I slept at home, or at least in my own town. One time, when Dad and Mom had to be gone for a few days, they took us kids out to Grandma Becksteads on the farm and left us there. Grandma was a sweet, motherly lady and very good to us, but by mid-afternoon I was determined to go home. It would soon be night and I was much too far from Bingham Canyon.

I began coaxing Don and Dottie to start walking home with me, or trying to "thumb" a ride, anything to get home before dark. But they wanted to stay at Grandma's and wouldn't listen to me. Then Aunt Ruby and Uncle Bob dropped in. They lived in Copperton, near the lower end of Bingham Canyon—and that was *almost* home. I asked Aunt Ruby if I could ride back and stay with her until the folks came home. She could see how much it meant to me, and figured I'd just as well stay with her as with Grandma, so agreed to take me. But when we reached her place I watched for a chance to slip away. Out on the road again, I caught a ride in short order and was soon back in my part of town.

When I got out of the car that had given me a lift, I headed straight for Riley's, marched through the bar to the cafe and told Barb my problem. She fed me, phoned Aunt Ruby to tell her where I was, and took me home with her and Riley that night. I didn't get to sleep in my own bed but I was back in the Knight Hotel when bedtime came.

Another time the folks sent me home with Grandma and Grandpa Lennon. I loved to go to their house—but not to stay all night. After a little while I began considering all kinds of ways to get home before night, but hadn't yet come up with a workable idea when Grandma said she had to go to a funeral that afternoon and that I'd have to go with her. At the church I recognized Woody, the undertaker from Bingham Canyon. He now and then had a funeral in Salt Lake, so I kept my eye on him and when the funeral was over I slipped up and asked him if he'd take me back to Bingham Canyon with him. Being one of my good friends, he said he would—if I didn't mind riding in the hearse.

Grandma was aghast at the idea of me riding home in *that* vehicle, but I begged so hard that she let me go. Of course I rode up in the front seat with Woody, but I wanted to go home so badly that I'd have ridden inside the hearse if I'd had to, or in a garbage truck, or *anything,* to get there. It was almost dark when we pulled up in front of the hotel—and nearly scared Mom into conniption fits when she saw the hearse stopping at her door.

Chapter Two

My Home

The Knight Hotel was a big building, long and rather narrow, its front flush with the main street sidewalk, its back hard against the steep mountain behind it. The front door opened into a big lobby furnished with a large registration desk, a long leather divan, some big leather chairs and several generous sized spittoons. The stairway to the upper floors went up from the lobby and, near the foot of it a wide doorway opened into the dining room. Our family parlor was just beyond that and the kitchen was at the back. A long hallway leading to the bedrooms extended from the lobby to the kitchen. The bedroom I shared with Dottie was first in line, then the bathroom, brother Don's room, and then Mom and Dad's room at the end.

I always had some good friends among the people who lived at the hotel, and it was a good thing, for I was always needing someone to do me a good turn, or get me out of trouble. I felt happy and secure as long as I was in my own bed at night and Mom and Dad were at home; but I panicked at the very thought of sleeping away from home and I was really upset if the folks were gone when bedtime came.

10

They went out in the evening once in a while, to dance or to visit friends, and then I was afraid to go to bed. Nothing bothered Dottie, who went right to sleep, but I lay awake in the dark and shivered and shook and imagined all kinds of scary things. I dreaded such nights so much that, one evening at bedtime, I went up to Herb, one of the men who worked in the mine daytimes and slept at the hotel nights, where he sat visiting in the lobby. I whispered my fears to him and asked if he'd mind staying in the lobby, with the door into the hall open, until the folks came home.

Herb said he wouldn't mind, and with him on guard I went right to sleep. But when Mom and Dad came in, very late, and found poor Herb dozing in his chair by the open door—and found out why—they were upset with me, and I was in trouble again.

Our parlor was quite elegant and we used it only for special occasions. The furniture, big tables and overstuffed chairs, was ornate and heavy and there was a fancy carved mantle over the fireplace. Mom was very particular about all her furniture and took very good care of it. Consequently Dottie and I were never allowed to put our feet on anything but the floor, there, or in any other room in the place.

Now some of our friends could bounce on their beds or davenports, and when we visited them we bounced with them, but that was taboo at our place. Naturally we longed to jump on our beds and bounce up and down. We finally figured that, if we took our shoes off and bounced on the beds when we knew Mom was out of the hotel, we could get away with it. So we took our chances and bounced on the beds now and then and did acrobatics for one another. It was great fun and we were sure that, as long as we had our shoes off, Mom would never know about it.

But one day we bounced so high and hard that we broke my bed down. The springs and mattress, everything, was on the floor and there was no way we could hide *that* from Mom— unless we could get it fixed before she came home. So I flew to the lobby for help. Good natured, good looking Joe Granes was the only hotel guest there and I begged him to come quick and fix my bed.

11

Joe laughed and said he'd try. With Dottie and me hovering over him in a panic, he worked fast and had the bed back together before Mom came home—and none of us ever breathed a word about it to her.

As far as I can remember there was only one person in all of Bingham Canyon who was *not* my friend and, though I tried and tried, I never won him over. He lived next door to the hotel, across the narrow alley that ran from the street to the retainer wall at the base of the mountain. His name was Henry and he lived alone. A short, husky, powerfully built man, he didn't want any friends and wouldn't let anyone come inside his gate or up onto his porch. A wealthy man, he didn't have to go to work, so was home all the time.

Strangely enough, he made one exception to his no visitors rule, and that exception was my sister Dottie. She was a plump, pretty, cute little two-year-old and he used to *call* to her to come onto his porch. Then he'd talk to her and give her cookies by the handful. I'd hang on the gate and grin at him and call "Hi, Hiney, Hi Hiney," (at four I couldn't say Henry) but he only scowled back and wouldn't answer me a word.

Dottie was soon trotting through the gate and into his house whenever she liked, and always came back with her hands full of cookies of different kinds. She'd then offer me one cookie, but I didn't get to pick it out. *She* did, and it was usually the one she didn't want.

Then we both got the measles and Mom bought us dark glasses and put us to bed, daytimes, in her room and made us wear the glasses until we were well again. One day Henry came knocking on the bedroom window and asked Mom if we could have candy. She said we could and he gave us *each* a sack and *laughed* at us, looking so owly in our big, dark glasses. That was the only time he ever treated us both alike, and not long after that he died.

Dottie and I loved to steal cherries from a neighbor farther down the street. Every summer for two or three years, after the cherries were ripe, we watched our chance and climbed the fence into his tiny back yard. Filling our mouths, pockets and hands, we then fled back over the fence to enjoy our loot, and well pleased with ourselves for getting away with it. Mr. Auble was a friendly man who would likely have given us all the cherries we wanted if we had asked him for them but it was more fun to steal them, and we probably thought they tasted better that way.

Then we got a little dog, Tiny, a toy terrier that went everywhere with us and was very special to me. When the cherries ripened again we made our usual raid, taking Tiny with us, boosting her over the fence and heading for the cherry tree. Before we'd more than gotten started picking fruit we saw Mr. Auble coming. We ran with all speed to the fence and jumped over—and then I saw Tiny, looking pleadingly up at me. Of course I jumped back in the yard to get her, and by then Mr. Auble was there.

He took us home and told our folks what we'd been up to and, as the oldest and, naturally, the leader, I got the hardest spanking. But I was always glad I'd gone back after Tiny. She was our friend and shared all our ice cream cones with us. We'd take a lick and she'd take a lick, right down to the last one.

There were few yards, or lawns, in the crowded canyon that made up our town and, of course, few outdoor flowers. I loved the few gay blossoms there were, and when I found that a friend of Mom's had a yard full of them I went up there often. Mrs. Glenn lived up on the mountain side almost directly above the hotel. To reach their home the Glenns, and a few other families that lived up on "the ridge," had to drive up Carr Fork, a little branch canyon, then make a sharp turn onto a gravel road that edged its way up the mountain side to the ridge that ran along the rim of the mine.

Mrs. Glenn lived in the first of a short row of pretty brick houses on the ridge, where she had a front yard filled with flowers. Instead of going around by the road I simply took a shortcut to her house, climbing like a goat up the mountain above the hotel to her yard, where I picked a handful of the pretty blooms to take home to Mom. After I'd helped myself a few times, Mrs. Glenn told my mother she wished I'd let her know when I wanted flowers, as she'd be glad to pick them for me—with stems on them instead of just the heads, the way I did it.

But I quit taking things that didn't belong to me after the

time Mom took Dottie and me with her on a shopping trip to Salt Lake City. In Woolworth's I saw a sparkling ring that I wanted, but when I asked Mom for it she said no. I almost always had the money for anything I wanted, or else Mom would buy it for me, but that day I had no money and Mom wasn't in the notion.

So I waited, and when she was busy with something else and no one was looking, I took the ring. I put it on my finger and wore it out to the car, trying to keep it covered so Mom wouldn't notice it. But she saw it and asked me how I got it. When I told her she marched me right back into the store and sent for the manager—and I had to give the ring back to him and tell him I was a thief. That cured me.

I almost always had plenty of money of my own when I was little, for it usually wasn't hard to come by. Before Grandpa and Grandma Lennon moved to Salt Lake they often gave me money, and they still did whenever they came back to visit us, or we went to see them. And the men at the hotel were always a good source, frequently giving me nickels and dimes. Pay days were the best times, though, and I made it a point to be on hand when Mom cashed their checks at the big desk. They'd turn away and see me sitting there and peel a dollar bill off the rolls in their fists and hand it to me. Most of them were single men and they always felt good on pay day.

Then, the summer I was five, I went into the ore business. Quite a few of the Bingham Canyon kids were in the business. It was a steady source of income during the summers; for by then a good many tourists were coming to the Canyon to get a look at the great pit at the top of the mountain above the town.

Even in those days the mammoth mine almost surrounded the canyon town and the Kennecott company had just completed its long one-lane tunnel through the mountain to another huge mine pit on the far side. On our side the mouth of the tunnel was directly across the street from our hotel and green and red stop and go lights regulated the traffic through the big bore.

The tunnel was soon a familiar place to me, but scary if I had to go through it alone. It had a sidewalk for foot travelers, and lights in the ceiling that shed a dim glow on the roadway. Even so, it was a shadowy, spooky place and when I had to travel it alone I ran most of its mile and a quarter length.

Tourists planning to go through the tunnel to look at the mine waited in the crowded parking space at our end for the oncoming traffic to clear and the light to turn green, and those waiting visitors were our potential customers. I'd walk among the vehicles, pick out a good looking car and offer to give the occupants a tour of the mine for fifty cents. I was almost always hired, tendered a half-dollar and invited to get in and ride.

I had already filled my pockets with shiny chunks of copper ore, and while we waited for the light to change I displayed my wares and usually sold some for two-bits a chunk. There was another parking space at the far end of the tunnel, where we got out and walked over to look at the tremendous hole in the mountain and watched the huge shovels scooping up the ore and loading it into trucks and trains to be hauled to the smelters and refineries.

While my carload of visitors oggled the mine, I was usually looking for more pieces of ore, which I picked up and slipped into my pockets to sell to the next carload of travelers. Then I'd ride back to the Bingham Canyon side with my tourists, get out and grab another waiting car. It was a good racket, and the tourists seemed to think they'd gotten their money's worth.

The big chartered buses were good sources of revenue, too. We couldn't ride through the tunnel in them—something about the insurance—but most of the drivers were friendly fellows who would let us kids get on the buses while they were parked and sell our ore to the passengers.

But if I was broke and needed money in a hurry—and if all else failed—I could always fall back on the piggy bank as a sure source of supply. The bank, a huge china pig about a foot high and very fat, belonged to Dad, who kept it on the mantle piece in the parlor. He had been putting his loose change into the bank for years and the pig was well-fed and heavy—but not as heavy as it should have been—for I had found out that if I laid the pig on its side and slid a knife blade into the coin slot I could bring out a coin or two at every try.

Then one day, in extreme need, I rushed to the parlor, made sure the coast was clear, and hefted the pig off the mantle. But before I could get off the stone hearth with it and onto the carpet I dropped the heavy animal. Coins and pieces of china scattered all over the floor. This time I'd really *done* it. I slipped silently away and waited miserably for the inevitable blow to fall.

Dad had had that china pig for a long time and thought a lot of it. When he learned of its demise he called us all together, Don, Dottie and me. He asked Dottie first, and then Don, if they had broken the pig. Since they were innocent their denials sounded sincere, so he turned to me. I knew he wouldn't believe me if I said I didn't know anything about it—and I was thinking fast. I thought my story was pretty good then, and I still think so. I told him I liked the old pig a lot too, and that I was just petting it when it fell off and broke.

That was the summer too, that I became Mom's bank runner. Every Saturday morning she banked an average of $500, the week's hotel receipts. I had sometimes gone to the bank with her, and had even gone with her into the private office of the president, Mr. Parsons.

One morning soon after I turned five, Mom was too busy to go to the bank, so she gave me the canvas sack of silver, bills and checks and told me to take it straight to the bank and make the deposit for her. Impressed with my importance as the carrier of so much money, I marched across the street and down a couple of doors to the First Security Bank.

Each Saturday morning there was a line of people at the cashier's window, waiting their turn to get to the taker and dispenser of cash. I had waited in that line with Mom on earlier occasions but I didn't intend to stand in it that morning. Not me. With a death grip on my money sack, I paraded right by the line and across the room on my way to Mr. Parsons' office.

The cashier saw me and the money sack and called out, "Better get on the end of the line, Betty Ann." I called back, "No thank you, I have business to do," and walked into Mr. Parsons' office. He looked surprised and asked what he could do for me. "I have business," I said, and handed him my sack. His eyes bagan to twinkle and he asked me to sit down while he took care of my "business."

He emptied the bag on his desk top and sorted and counted

and made a list of its contents. He put the receipt in the sack and handed it back to me, then visited a little while. After that, every Saturday morning for a long time I took the hotel receipts to the bank for Mom, and each time I went right by the line at the window and into Mr. Parsons' office, and each time he treated me with the deference due the important customer I thought I was, while he counted the money and filled out the deposit slip.

Before I was old enough to go to school I'd had one thumb and both my pinkie fingers broken. We used to get woven straw finger-stalls in boxes of cracker jacks. The little gadgets were loose, floppy things that we slipped onto our little fingers, but when we tried to pull them off we were in a fix. The harder we pulled the tighter they stuck. The trick was to release all pressure from the top, or closed end, and push them off from the bottom.

I broke my left pinkie trying to get the first one off. Mom took me to Dr. Frazier, who put a cast on the finger. A day or so later I got another of the straw gadgets out of another box of cracker jacks, put it on my other little finger—and broke that one too, trying to get the thing off. Mom said I never learned anything from experience as she marched me back to the doctor, who put a cast on that finger, too.

I couldn't seem to leave the casts alone. Before Mom knew what I was doing I had them both off. Back at the doctor's, he considered the matter and said he didn't think it would do any good to put new casts on. So both of my little fingers are crooked to this day.

I broke my thumb when I ran into Casey, the handyman at Big Helen's 520 place. Casey was the only name I ever knew for him. A very shy, quiet fellow, he was always friendly and kind to me. A short, dumpy, dark little man, he wore glasses and seemed always to have a mop or a broom in his hand; as his main work at the 520 was keeping the place clean, though he also ran errands and carried the groceries home from the store.

Bingham Canyon had a fine, modern fire department, manned entirely by volunteer fire fighters. Most of the men in town were volunteers, prepared at all times to drop whatever they were doing and dash to the fire house to man the hose wagon and head for the fire. With so many wooden buildings in the town, and all so close together, there were a good many fires. Casey, one of the volunteers, loved his job and never missed a fire, although the whole town chuckled over the way he showed up at every fire with his mop or his broom in his hand.

Dad gave me a new red coaster wagon, that last summer before I started to school and, first thing, I pulled it up the street quite aways, climbed in and took off down the steep sidewalk, steering by the upturned handle. I was doing fine until I got to going so fast that it scared me. The first opening off the sidewalk was a narrow space between the 520 and Nick's place. I knew I'd have to turn in there to stop, and I knew I'd have to stop right away or I'd have a wreck, but just as I started to turn in Casey stepped into that space, his mop over his shoulder.

It was too late for me to turn back. "Look out! Look out!" I screamed at him, but he didn't move. Either there wasn't time, or he couldn't think fast enough to jump out of the way. Anyway I hit him, head on. Poor fellow, his leg had all the skin scraped off of it and his knee was badly banged up—and I had a broken thumb.

Chapter Three

My Home Town

Like a pudding poured into a mould, the town of Bingham Canyon had to fit its location—a long, winding, narrow canyon that gashed the side of a high mountain in the Oquirrh Range, 28 miles southwest of Salt Lake City. The town's single street ran up the middle of the canyon and was lined solidly on both sides with business buildings, hotels, apartment houses and homes. Side by side and almost stacked on top of each other, it almost seemed that the roof of one building was the front porch for the one above it.

The front doors abutted on the narrow sidewalks, the rear ends thrust against the mountain side. Bingham Canyon people claimed their street was seven miles long and only forty feet wide—too narrow for the town dogs to wag their tails sideways, so they wagged them up and down. The lower end of the canyon opened onto the valley in the village of Lead Mine; the upper end came to a stop at the main pit of the Kennecott Copper Mines. Before they built the tunnel the road had gone on over the top of the mountain and down into the village of Copperfield.

On the right side of Bingham Canyon two short canyons, Freeman Gulch and Carr Fork, branched off to other parts of the mine. The upper gulch, Carr Fork, was the longest and, angling off the main canyon as it did, gave the town a Y shape. The upper end of the Fork, just beyond a turn in the canyon, was known as Highland Boy, named for a mine located there in 1873, probably by a Scotsman.

At the lower end of the canyon the little town of Lead Mine had grown up around the big, smokey ore smelters and their dusty slag piles. A village in its own right, it had its own bar, cafe and a few homes. Just above it was the tight little Greek section known as "Frogtown." The Greeks had their own bars, cafes, grocery stores, barber shops and garages, two breweries, a pool hall, bakeries, a large apartment house and numerous small homes.

Next to Frogtown was a short, desolate stretch of rocky canyon with the narrow road hugging its bottom. Railroad tracks, like cramped shelves built on high trestles, followed the mountains on either side. Little ore trains shuttled back and forth on the winding tracks, hauling ore from the mines to the smelters and clanging back up the canyon with the empties.

Bingham Canyon proper began with more bars, cafes and homes intermixed on either side of the street. Next, on the left, stood the big American Legion Civic Center, more houses, cafes and a bar or two, and then the Bingham Central Grade School where Dottie and I learned our three R's, along with most of the town's Greek children and those of several other nationalities.

On the right side of the street there was a garage and more homes and then the fire station, tucked into the V where Freeman Gulch angled off from Main, just across from the school.

Just above the schoolhouse a car dealer's garage and a butcher shop flanked the Post Office. In the early days, so I was told, mail for everybody except the box renters was tossed onto a counter where each patron looked through the pile for anything addressed to him, or just to see who else in town had gotten some mail. Later Uncle Sam hired a postman who rode horseback up the street with the mail in saddle bags and delivered it where it belonged. By my time the town had paved its street and the mailman could make it all the way to the top in a Ford car.

The Number 2 drug store snuggled between the post office and the Bingham Hospital, where Dr. Paul Richards was in charge. Across the street the Ford garage fitted into the angle on the upper side of Freeman Gulch, alongside the Copper Hospital, owned by the U. S. mine and managed by Dr. Russell Frazier. The J. C. Penney store came next, and then a Greek shoemaker's shop. From there, on up to Carr Fork, there was another cafe and bar, next to the Princess Theatre and the Pastime Cafe, owned by a Chinese family who served delicious Oriental food.

The Catholic Recreation Hall was next to the Bingham Hospital, beside the Number 1 drug store. The Evans brothers owned and operated the two drug stores. Earl tended one and Bob the other. There was a big boarding house above the Number 1, then a second-hand store and two high class bars, the Diamond and the Big Four.

The Bingham Mercantile Company general store fronted on Bingham Canyon at its intersection with Carr Fork. The biggest store in town, it seemed almost a block square and, due to the steeply climbing street, was built on two levels. Its front, or Main Street, door opened into the drygoods and clothing department, where, from its many aisles and counters, one could buy shoes, shirts, dresses, underwear, hats, caps, hose, gloves, jewelry, ribbons, yard goods, bedding and dozens of other things.

The sidewalk in front of the Bingham Merc was wider than the walk above or below it and had a roof over it, making a kind of porch or platform where band concerts, street shows and various kinds of speakers performed. Sixteen wooden steps led from the end of the porch down to the corner of the building on the Carr Fork side. I know there were sixteen because I fell down them so often that I was familiar with every one of them.

The Merc had a street door at the back, another opening onto Carr Fork, and a steep stairway inside that funneled folks down from the upper floor to the grocery part where a sizable space had a butcher on duty. From the sides and quarters of meat hanging on his rails the butcher cut any size and quantity and kind of meat the buyer fancied. At the back of that lower floor was a big hardware and furniture section. About the only thing the Merc didn't sell was coffins. My friend Woody handled that business.

The Bingham Merc owner, Charles Adderley, a kind and genial man, was another of my good friends. He and Mrs. Adderley had a beautiful home a few blocks below the store, where an ornate iron fence enclosed the yard-wide strip of lawn in front of their house.

Above the Merc, on Main Street, the Butte Club came next. It was one of the town's fanciest bars, and beside it was Big Helen's 520 place. Nick's tailor shop was next, then the telephone office and then my home, the Knight Hotel. On the other side of the street, above the Big Four, were some more stores, apartments, a barber shop and then the bank, with the Police Station between it and the entrance to the big tunnel.

The canyon widened a bit above the mouth of the tunnel and they had made use of that bit of extra space to pave a parking lot, the only one we had, so cars could park off the street while waiting to drive through the mountain. The Mexican cafe was just above the tunnel, then the Bingham Hotel, the Copper Hotel and the big Japanese boarding house. The Canyon Hotel, perched almost on the rim of the mine, was the last building on that side of the street.

On the other side, the Belmont Hotel faced the Bingham. Crowded in beside it was an old "variety store," forerunner of the dime stores that were fast replacing them, and then a string of apartment houses all the way back down to the Knight Hotel.

The Finns and Swedes congregated in Freeman Gulch (so named for the Freeman brothers who had died in a cave-in of their mine at its upper end in the early days). Apartment houses and homes lined both sides of the Gulch, with little frame structures, much like old-time privies, tucked in behind them. The Scandinavians took steam baths in the little huts. The baths were quite a lot of work, for they had to first heat rocks very hot and then throw cold water on them to make the steam. The miners especially enjoyed the baths after they came off their daily shifts in the mines. The apartment houses and hotels had their own built-in steam rooms and the price of using them was included in the room rental.

Carr Fork was longer, and much more interesting, than Freeman Gulch. It began with the Copper King bar, just across the street from the side door of the Bingham Merc. Up to where it made the sharp turn, the street was mostly Greek; there was a Greek grocery store, barber shops, cafes, apartment houses and homes. At the upper end of the canyon the big Gemmell Club building stood on one side of the street, the little Catholic church on the other, right where the tracks of the tramway, standing almost on end, took off up the side of the mountain. Little tram cars clanked up and down the two sets of tracks, providing passage up to the four story brick office of the mine company, and to the railroad tracks that ran to the mines.

Copperfield, at the end of the tunnel on the other side of the mountain, was mostly Greek, too. Another village of bars, cafes, boarding houses and small homes, all perched on the steep mountain side. The great open pits of the Kennecott dropped away from the upper side of its main street, which ended at the entrance to the underground section of the mine.

The Chinese lived in small shacks niched into the mountain above the buildings that lined the streets, both in Bingham Canyon and Copperfield. They were polite friendly people and I got along well with them. In fact, as far as race was concerned, all the kids in the mine towns got along fine. However, Copperfield had its own grade school so I didn't get to know the kids there so very well until they came over to our side to go to Junior High School.

In addition to the large colonies of Finns, Swedes, Greeks, Italians, Austrians, Slavs, Chinese and Japanese, we had Russians, Jews, Germans, Irish and other nationalities in our town. As far as I can remember, the only ones we didn't have when I lived there were Negroes and Indians, although I was told that a black teamster once made his home in Freeman Gulch and, so it was said, had associated with whites on equal terms for so long that he had forgotten he was a Negro.

Even with all those nationalities living there, Bingham Canyon was never a melting pot. Even though everybody associated with everybody else and did business with each other, each colony had its own stores, churches and barber shops, and each celebrated its own national holiday. But when it came to school and entertainment all the races mixed companionably. Although there were separate grade schools in Freeman, Carr Fork, Bingham Canyon and Copperfield, the kids simply went to the one nearest their homes, while everyone went to the Princess, the only theatre in town, and to Galena Days and the Fourth of July celebrations. It seemed that, while everyone was loyal to his own nationality, all of us considered ourselves *Americans*.

Looking back on it now, I know that it was a drab and dirty town, with dust from the mines and smelters hanging in the air; and almost no green lawns or trees. Just rocks and bare slopes and weathered little houses climbing the mountain sides. It must have looked even worse before my time, before they paved the street in 1928, for then, the folks told me, the usually dusty street turned into one long, deep mud puddle when it rained.

So that was the town I grew up in, and by the time I was five years old I knew it all, every turn of the steep street, every building from its shacks to its elegant Gemmell Club, City Hall, fire station and the big Bingham Merc. And for all the years that I lived there I knew most of its permanent residents.

To me the foreign languages that I heard every day, on the streets and in the stores and homes, were commonplace. I might wonder what the queer sounding words meant, the Scandinavian, the Serbian, Greek, Spanish, Chinese, Japanese, Armenian and all the others, but I could still communicate with all of them—by friendly smiles and gestures if nothing else.

I didn't know it then, but growing up in Bingham Canyon was, in a way, like growing up in Hong Kong or any other great crossroads city of the world would have been; for men and women from around the globe mingled on its narrow street and plied their trades there. Every day was interesting and exciting.

24

Chapter Four

My Family

There were just the five of us in my family, Mom and Dad, Don, Dottie and me. In the summers Don stayed out at Grandma Beckstead's farm, where he had lived as a little boy before Mom and Dad were married. He loved it out there and was a big help to Grandma with her gardens and orchards. So Dottie and I were on our own then, but when he came back to town for the school year he was a big help to us. We could tell him things and ask him questions that we didn't want to go to the folks with, and he always tried to help us. We loved him and looked up to him but, occasionally, we gave him a bad time too, like the times when we went for Sunday afternoon auto rides.

Mom and Dad rode in the front seat, of course, and we always started out with Dottie between Don and me in the back. But invariably, before we were even two miles down the street, Dottie and I were fighting—and always over the same thing. She'd be demanding to change places with me and sit next the window, and I wouldn't let her.

I can't remember that we *ever* got all the way out of town before Dad pulled the car over to the side of the road as far as

R. J. and Donna Contratto—
as they looked at the time of
the marriage in the early 30's.

Betty and her brother Donald.

My brother Don.

Betty at age two.

he could and got out and gave us each a spanking. Then he'd make Don sit in the middle, with Dottie on one side and me on the other. That made Don unhappy as he thought that, being the oldest, he should have a window seat, but he never gave the folks any trouble about it.

Instead, just before starting out, he'd beg Dottie and me to please be good, this time, and try to get along. We'd promise him we would, and we did try, but it never did any good. When he saw that it was hopeless, Don took to bringing funny books along to read after Dottie and I had had our spankings.

One Christmas Eve when we were quite small Dad and Mom, after sending us all to bed, went out for the evening. But we couldn't sleep and kept getting up to look in the parlor—Don to see if the folks were home yet, Dottie and I to see if Santa had come to leave our presents under the tree. Finally Don told us that, if we didn't go to sleep Santa wouldn't leave anything but coal in our stockings, as he didn't like to be watched while he worked.

That worried us, for not only did we want nice presents but we didn't want our friends to know that we had been so bad that coal was all we got. So we got into our beds and tried hard to go to sleep, but before we could manage it we heard the folks in the parlor. We got up again and opened the door a crack—and there were Dad and Mom, putting lovely presents under the tree and in our stockings for us. We caught on, *then*, that *they* were Santa Claus; but we were so glad to be getting nice presents instead of coal that we didn't really care.

The room where Dottie and I slept, the largest bedroom on the first floor, didn't have any outside windows, just an airshaft from the roof two stories above us to the ground floor, and our one window opened into that. Across the narrow shaft another window opened into Don's room, and Dottie and I often hopped through our window, crossed the shaft and climbed through Don's window for a visit or to ask advice, and Don sometimes came across to talk to us. His room had an outside door that opened onto the little alley that ran between our house and Henry's, ending against the mountain behind the hotel. Don's outside door was to come in handy for me when I got older.

Dottie and I were very different. I was daring, but never aggressive, and I always shunned any kind of physical combat; not so much because I was afraid of being hurt but more because I didn't want to hurt anyone else. I couldn't bear the thought of inflicting pain on anybody—even kids I was mad at. But not Dottie. She'd tie into anyone, no matter how much bigger they were, and I don't believe she'd have been afraid to tackle a cyclone with a knitting needle. So, although Dottie usually fought *my* battles for me, she also beat up on me, too, though she wouldn't let anyone else do it.

Our father was a strict disciplinarian who demanded respect from his children, and also instant obedience. One evening at the supper table, that last summer before I started to school, I was gobbling my food as fast as I could so I could go out and play with my friends. Dad told me to slow down and not eat so fast. I knew I had to mind, and I didn't dare "talk back." So all I could do to express my feelings was to stick my tongue out at him—but just the tip of it, so he wouldn't see it.

But I must have stuck out more than I meant to, for he did see it—and I knew I'd better get to moving. I was out of my chair in a flash, and out the door and down the street, with Dad right behind me. Boy! Could he run! Of course he caught me, and I was not only spanked but I didn't get to go out to play at all that evening.

From then on I understood why Dad had been such a great football player when he was in Bingham Canyon High, and why some of his friends still chanted the cheer they had made up for him when he was a senior:

Cheer boys, Cheer!
For Bunnie's got the ball.
Watch that guy,
He never takes a fall.
And when he hits that line,
There'll be no line at all.
There'll be a hot time in the old town tonight!

But Dad wasn't always a disciplinarian. I can remember wonderful summer dawns when he came off the night shift at the mine and wakened Dottie and me. He'd hurry us into our clothes and take us up Butterfield Canyon, a wild, steep gash in the mountainside, with little open meadows along the stream that tumbled down to Bingham Canyon. There we'd hide in the brush and watch the deer and elk come down from the higher slopes to feed and water by the creek. The air was so crisp and fresh, the birds spilling their sparkling songs all over, and the whole thing so beautiful that it was unforgettable. Those are the times that I remember far better than our spankings.

Somewhere along in there Dad quit the mine and became Chief of Police of Bingham Canyon. He was a good one, highly respected by our townspeople, and I was awfully proud of him. His police car was a black Pontiac sedan. Dad called it "Iron Mike," and every now and then took me and some of my friends along when he was cruising around in it. Sometimes the lights went out in the tunnel, or the stop lights at the ends went on the blink. Dad would take us along in Iron Mike at such times when he was looking for the trouble, driving with the siren screaming, and so fast that I'd scoot down in the seat so I couldn't see, and cover my ears so I couldn't hear.

Another difference between Dottie and me was the way we reacted to our many spankings. Dad spanked us until we said we were sorry for whatever we'd done that displeased him. Anyway that was the idea, and it worked with me. I'd yell that I was sorry by about the second whack, but not Dottie. When we were both spanked for the same misdeed, I'd get mine over in a hurry and then stand by, crying and begging, "Say you're sorry, Dottie, say you're sorry," but she wouldn't. She just took it until Dad gave up.

In spite of all our quarreling, Dottie and I had some good times together, like jumping on our beds, and some fun adventures such as swiping cherries from the neighbor's tree. But we seemed to disagree more often than we agreed. One of our differences was over our daily doses of cod-liver oil. I hated the stuff but Dottie actually liked it. Mom usually gave it to us just before she sent us to bed but sometimes, busy as she was with her hotel duties, she forgot it.

I was happy when that happened—but that Dottie, she'd go to bed as if she'd forgotten too, and lie there for awhile, like she wasn't going to remind Mom. And then, just when I thought she'd gone to sleep and I had it made for that one night, anyway, she'd yell, "Mom, you forgot our cod-liver oil."

Our beds were on opposite sides of our big bedroom, as far apart as we could get them, but even so I was often wakened in the night by my sister pounding on me with her shoe. She couldn't stand to hear anybody breathe and she'd wake me up to tell me she could hear me breathing, and that I had to stop it. She has always been like that, and when she married she took to wearing ear plugs so she couldn't hear her husband breathe.

Chapter Five

My School Days

I passed my fifth birthday in April, and all that summer I was eager to start school. It would be a new experience—and I loved new experiences.

In September the big day came. I had planned to go down the street to Bingham Central Grade school all by myself, but Mom told me she was going to walk to school with me, that first day. I didn't want her to, as I knew I was big enough to go by myself, but she went anyway.

I had a new dress and new shoes and pretty white anklets. I had a fancy new tin lunch bucket too, and I felt mighty important as we walked past Nick's place, and Big Helen's and the Bingham Merc, and past Carr Fork and the Pastime, but I'd have felt a lot more important if Mom had let me go alone. Then, as we came closer to the schoolhouse, my courage and importance began to seep away. By the time we came to Penney's, the hospital and the fire station I was feeling pretty shaky. I was glad Mom was with me by the time we walked into the kindergarden room, where Mom introduced me to the teacher, and then left me. The minute she was out of sight I folded up and bawled. I had never felt so forsaken and alone in my life, and I couldn't understand a mother who would go off and leave her little girl like that.

Dottie, of course, had wanted to go to school with me, and felt awfully left out because she couldn't. To stop her fussing Dad bought her a new tricycle. After I'd been in school a few days and the new had worn off, I decided it would be more fun to stay home and help Dottie ride her tricycle. She was pretty good about letting me take turns, one of us pedaling and the other riding on the bar behind.

Since the folks wouldn't let me stay out of school just to ride the tricycle, I had to begin thinking up good reasons for staying home. The only possible way, I found, was to be too sick to go to school. But after trying that a time or two—and then getting well soon after school started and riding with my sister on the cycle, Mom didn't fall for that one anymore. I kept on trying, though, and thinking up all kinds of new symptoms. But nothing worked.

And then one morning I really was sick, too sick to eat any breakfast, and my stomach felt terribly queasy and erpy. But Mom, sure I was faking, didn't even bother to feel my forehead. "You're going to school," she said, "and that's all there is to it." So I left the hotel by the front door—and threw up on the sidewalk in front of the door.

Mom was in the kitchen, so didn't see that, and by then I was mad at her anyway—a mother would wouldn't let her little girl stay home from school when she was so awfully sick—so, to punish her, I decided I'd just go on to school.

Dr. Frazier was at the school that morning, vaccinating the kids in the fourth grade for something, and when I dragged upstairs to my room the teacher took one look at me, then felt my hot forehead and sent me down to the fourth grade room.

The doctor felt me and prodded me for a few minutes, then called Mom and told her I had an acute attack of appendicitis and that he would advise them to take me to Salt Lake City right away, where he would meet them at the hospital and operate immediately.

I was well satisfied with Mom's contrition over the whole affair and, after I got over being nauseated from the ether, I had a fine time. Dad and Mom came to see me every day and the nurses made such a fuss over me that I felt like a queen all the time I was there. At home it was great, too. Dottie waited on me hand and foot and the boarders paid me lots of attention. I made it last as long as I could, but all too soon I was well again and back in school, my center-of-the-stage importance a thing of the past.

Another trial of that year, and for several years to come, was the long, ribbed brown cotton stockings Mom bought me. As soon as the weather turned cold she made me wear them, instead of my neat, stylish white anklets. Most of the other girls went on wearing their white anklets all winter, so the few of us who had to wear the ugly long stocking overcame our mortification to some extent by rolling, or folding, the long stockings down to our shoetops as soon as we were out of sight of our homes. Then, except for their color, they did not look so different from out schoolmates' anklets. On the way home in the afternoon we pulled them up again and showed up before our mothers looking the way they expected us to.

Mom was a stickler for those long stocking and I had to wear them during cold weather for as long as I went to school in Bingham Canyon. To all my protests and tears she replied that she wasn't going to have me catching my death of cold, or developing a bad case of rheumatism in my legs that would last all my life.

I behaved myself in school fairly well for the first three or four years, except that I'll always be ashamed of one stunt I pulled. Our art teacher was a kind little old man, bald-headed and weak-eyed, who wore glasses and seemed kind of timid. One day he went into the closet behind his desk where his art supplies were stored. I had noticed there was a lock on the door and, quick as a flash, I shot out of my seat, slammed the door and turned the lock. And *then,* while he called and called to us to let him out, I fished his lunch pail out from under his desk and divided its contents with the rest of the class. We had finished eating his lunch by the time the dismissal bell rang, when I unlocked the door and left the room with the rest of the kids.

When I saw him a little later he looked as if he had been

crying, and then I began to be ashamed of myself. Much later, after I found that I was claustrophobic and couldn't bear to be shut into an elevator or any other small space, I wondered if the little art teacher might have suffered the same way, shut up in that tiny, dark room. So far as I know, he never reported that schoolroom incident to anyone.

Otherwise, school wasn't so bad until I got into the fifth grade. My English teacher, that year, was Miss Baier. Now my brother Don, who had been her pupil before me, was very, very good at English and she seemed to think it should run in the family. But English was one of my worst subjects and I couldn't satisfy Miss Baier at all. She was always saying, "Betty, *why* can't you learn English the way your brother did?" I couldn't seem to do anything about it and I came to dread that class.

The sixth grade was much worse, for there I had a teacher who was a strict disciplinarian. For one thing she couldn't stand gum chewing and it was absolutely prohibited in her hall and classroom. Now I loved to chew gum, and one day during the first week of school I forgot the rule and put a fresh stick of gum in my mouth just before we were called in from our lunch hour. I didn't want to waste it by throwing it away so soon, so figured that, if I watched the teacher and didn't chew while she was looking in my direction, I could get away with it.

Of course I got interested in something else and forgot to watch the teacher and she caught me. After making me put the gum in the waste basket she told me I would be disciplined at recess—and left me to wonder what she'd do to me then. Since I was the first one to be caught I didn't think about much else for the next hour or so—when I found out. She had retrieved my gum from the waste basket and, just before dismissing the class for recess, she made me stick it on the end of my nose and stand in the hall, where all my classmates marched past me, giggling at my predicament.

I hated to be laughed at, but before the year was over most of the class had suffered the same indignity; for the punishment was the same for everybody and hardly anyone escaped her sharp eyes if chewing gum "illegally."

That teacher couldn't stand for any fooling around in the

classroom either, and she was death on tardiness. Anyone who misbehaved in class, or came in late, had to wait until recess, her favorite punishment time, and then sit on a high stool in the hall outside the classroom door and wear a tall dunce hat. Of course all the other kids went by, tittering and smirking, and the "dunce" felt awful. At least I did. It happened to me only a few times, and each time I made up my mind that I'd *never* have to do it again. Either I'd be so good that the teacher would have no reason to punish me, or I'd be so careful that I wouldn't get caught. But I'd get careless after awhile and, before I knew it, I'd be wearing the dunce hat again.

Long before the end of that year I was eager to get into Junior High. It would not only get me out of the reach of that sixth grade martinet, but I'd be riding the school bus for the first time, and going to a different school in a different town.

In 1931, when Bingham Canyon outgrew its small high school, the people of Highland Boy, Copperfield, Bingham Canyon, Lark and Copperton banded together and built a big new high school in Copperton, four or five miles from the mouth of Bingham Canyon. Lark, a few miles south of Copperton, was a small village of about the same size. The population of the five towns totaled about 6,000 at the time and, by combining and arranging to run buses from all the little municipalities, a large school building, complete with a fine gymnasium, was possible. Classes from the seventh grade through the twelfth attended the school.

The new school was fine and I liked going there, but I still had a problem—a big girl who rode the same school bus I did. She was bigger than I was, and alwasy trying to pick a fight with me. I wouldn't fight, and tried to pay no attention to her. Finally she took to threatening me when the bus stopped at the hotel door to pick me up, making like she wasn't going to let me get on it. This went on for several days and I began to dread the arrival of the bus, although she always backed off at the last minute and let me by her.

Now the bus driver never interferred with the kids on his bus, nor mixed into their many squabbles. He just pretended not to notice and I knew I could not depend on him for any help. Then one morning Mable didn't back up. "You're not getting on this bus," she snapped at me, and stood solidly in the door, barring my way.

When I saw that she really didn't mean to let me on, I began to bawl at the top of my voice and ran back into the hotel. Dottie, who was in the lobby, gathering up her books and lunch pail to hike down the street to Bingham Central, was out of the door like a flash and onto the step of that bus. Mable was a lot the biggest, but Dottie was strong and determined and very angry. She simply dragged that surprised big girl off the bus and pounded her up pretty good.

While that was going on I hurried into the bus and took my seat. When Dottie finished with Mable and let her go she got onto the bus too, quite subdued, and let me alone. She never gave me any trouble after that and, later, we became very good friends.

On the whole, my year in the seventh grade was a pretty good one, even though I was temporarily expelled before it was over. Now and then I was bored with school, or simply wanted a bit of change, so I took to skipping classes for a couple of periods; sometimes by myself, but usually with one or two of my girl friends. We called it "sluffing school," and it usually happened on a fine day when we couldn't bear to be shut up in the school room, or at a time when one or another of us had a difficult assignment that we wanted to "put off" as long as possible.

We'd spend the time climbing the mountain above the town, or just fooling around in the Bingham Merc, looking at things and keeping a sharp lookout for any of our parents. We could always tell our teachers that we had been sick, or helping our mothers, and it worked fine until the last time.

Late in the spring I proposed that we sluff school for a whole day. There were three of us in on it and, before we'd decided just what we'd do all day, one of the girls found out that some older kids were driving up to Salt Lake City for the day. We asked to go along and they agreed to take us. One of my friends had a girl friend who went to school in Salt Lake and we could spend the day with her.

The Salt Lake girl showed us around her school that forenoon and introduced us to her city friends, then went with us at noon to get something to eat. By that time we had talked her into sluffing her own school for the afternoon, so we walked around town and went into stores and looked at things and had a great time, then met the older kids for the ride back to Bingham Canyon. We showed up at our homes at the usual after school hour—and thought we'd gotten away with the whole deal as slick as a whistle.

But the next morning when we got to school we found out we were in deep trouble. One of the teachers had seen us getting into the older kids' car and, when we didn't show up for classes, had figured out what was going on. First, the principal, Mr. McMullin, called us into his office and gave us a real talking to. It was Friday and he told us we were *expelled* until the next Tuesday, and then we could come back only if we brought notes from our parents, stating that they knew what we had done, and why we couldn't go to school on Monday.

So we faced the music at home—and then came back to school with our notes on Tuesday morning, where we learned that our punishment wasn't over yet. Mr. McMullin had called a special assembly of the whole school in order to use us as a good example of what happens to students who break the rules. He made us get up before all the kids and tell what we had done and why we had to miss school on Monday, and then present him the notes from our parents and tell him how sorry we were for skipping school. The humiliation was awful, and that was the end of my sluffing school days.

Chapter Six

The Princess Theater

In my time Bingham Canyon had only one movie theater, the Princess. The first Princess had burned down the year I was born, along with a large section of Highland Boy. After the fire Mr. Ted Chesler, a Jewish man, established and operated the Princess I knew, and when he died his son Harold took over the business.

A strange custom prevailed at the matinees, when the audience was mostly all kids. The kids who lived on Bingham Canyon's long main street sat in the big middle section of the auditorium, the kids from Highland Boy sat in the section on the left and those from Copperfield in the section on the right. If it was an attempt at some sort of segregation it was the only one I ever knew about in the town; but it seemed to be a rigid, though unwritten, rule. Even if I went there with one of my best friends, and she was from Highland Boy or Copperfield, as soon as we were past the door she went to her section and I went to mine. We never understood why it was that way, but we never questioned the custom.

There was a matinee every afternoon and the regular show

in the evening. The matinees cost a nickel, the evening shows a dime. They changed the show once a week, on Saturdays, and I hardly ever missed a show, afternoon or evening, as there wasn't any other kind of regular entertainment in the town. The first few times I saw a show I could find something new in it each additional time I saw it, something I'd missed during the other runs, but toward the end of the week I became so familiar with the story that I knew exactly what was coming next, every word, act and gesture, and it began to be boring.

About that time Mom sent me to dancing school, where I learned to tap dance. I always did like to sing and clown around, and so, after a few lessons, I thought I was pretty good. One evening, after I was tired of the old show that I'd seen about ten times, I hustled up on the stage and put on my own act, singing and tapping. The kids in the three sections, most of them as bored as I was, began to clap their hands and stamp their feet and holler. The grownups weren't so appreciative; some of them hadn't seen the current episode of the Perils of Paulene and didn't care for the interruption.

After a few minutes Mr. Chesler, from up in his projection cubicle under the roof, shouted at me to get off the stage. But I was having fun and he was a long ways away, so I kept on singing Suwannee River and tapping like mad. Not until Mr. Chesler left his projection booth and started down the stairs did I give up and run out the back door.

My friends had enjoyed my part of the entertainment so much and urged me to keep on with it, that almost every week after that, when we were tired of the same old show, I pranced up on the stage and danced my newest steps and sang my latest song. I stopped only when the manager came down from his perch and was halfway up the aisle.

Later I turned out to be a pretty good tap dancer and my teacher teamed me with a boy named John and we danced for different clubs and civic groups in Bingham Canyon and our folks were very proud of us. I also played the accordian and was in good demand as an entertainer at town affairs and was even scheduled a time or two to dance in programs on the stage at the Princess. I really enjoyed that, for it was my opportunity to smirk triumphantly at Mr. Chesler, who had chased me off that stage so many times.

I was always easily frightened at night, or in the dark, and when they showed a spooky picture at the Princess I'd get so scared I could hardly breathe. Such shows never bothered Dottie—they just gave her new ideas for scaring me, such as slipping away from the crowd when we left the theater and running up the street to hide in the space between Nick's and the 520. When I came along she'd jump out at me and make strange, hideous noises. Frightened as I was already, I'd go right into a fit of the screaming meamies and run for home as hard as I could go, yelling at the top of every leap.

One night there was a particularly scary show, a Frankenstein picture, and after a little I couldn't bear to watch it any longer. I was also too scared to go home by myself and Dottie wouldn't go with me, so I got down under the seat and stayed there through the rest of the show. When it was over everyone left but me. Maybe my sister had forgotten that I hadn't gone home already. Anyway, she left, too.

I was too frightened to leave my dark little space under the seat, even when Mr. Chesler turned out the lights and left. I just hunkered there in the dark, shivering and almost suffocated from terror. After awhile someone came in and began hunting around with a flashlight and calling my name. It sounded like Dad but I couldn't be sure—it might be Frankenstein pretending to be my father. I almost quit breathing and hugged the floor tighter than ever.

Finally Dad got down on his hands and knees and began crawling between the rows of seats, flashing the light from side to side. But not until he was close enough that I could actually *see* him did I believe that he was really my father and that I dared to come out. By then I was so stiff and warped from all that time under the seat that I could hardly straighten out and stand up.

One time, after we were both in school, Dottie and I went to the library on a Saturday afternoon, and then to the show, carrying our books with us. After we were in our seats Dottie got upset with me over something and hit me a whack with a book, just below my right ear. I left the show, bawling, and ran home to tell Mom. She looked me over but couldn't find any mark, so told me to forget it and it would soon stop hurting. It probably already had—but when I got up the next morning I had a horrible swelling beneath that ear. I ran to Mom, full of righteous triumph, and showed her. "See," I said, "Dottie really hurt me bad when she hit me with the book."

It did look serious, so Mom sent for Dr. Frazier. He came, looked at the swelling and made me yelp when he prodded it with his fingers. Then he began to laugh. "Donna," he said to Mom, "I don't think you have anything to worry about. This girl just has a good case of the mumps."

I think I was in the fifth grade when a Bingham Canyon boy named Harold asked me to go to the show with him. I was embarrassed and didn't know what to tell him, as I really didn't want to go to the show with a "date." I didn't know what you were supposed to do on a date, and was sure the way it had always been, just the whole bunch of us going and each one paying his own way, was the best.

I didn't have the "nerve" to tell Harold no, so I thought fast and told him he'd have to ask Mom. I didn't think she'd let me go, and she could be the one to tell him no. Well, he asked her and she said I could, but that we'd have to go to the matinee, not an evening show.

Harold called for me that afternoon and we walked down the street to the Princess and it wasn't so bad. We talked, just like always, and I even felt a little important as Harold handed over the two nickels for our tickets. We picked out seats in the center section and got settled, and then the lights went down and the movie began. Everything still went well—for awhile— and then Harold reached over and tried to hold my hand.

From the uncertain way he fumbled I've no doubt he was as embarrassed as I was. He probably thought he was supposed to, and that I expected it of him. It was too much for me. I pulled my hand away, told him I had to go to the bathroom and fled. I ran straight home and told Mom what had happened— and didn't exactly know how to take it when she laughed.

Later in the afternoon, after the movie was over, Harold showed up again. He explained to Mom that his mother had given him money for ice cream, too, for after the show, and that he was supposed to take me to the drug store to eat it and could I go with him now to get it. Mom said I could, only it would have to be tomorrow as it was now too late, too near supper time. So Harold came back the next day and we had the ice cream, and so finished our date. He never asked me for another, and neither did anyone else until I was old enough to handle such occasions.

Since there was no flat, or even mildly sloping playground space in Bingham Canyon, all of us kids became expert mountain climbers and spent a lot of our time scampering around on the nearly vertical sides of the mountains that enclosed our town. But one couldn't play baseball on a mountain side, so we used our one street for a ball field.

Of course I played ball with the rest of the town kids and there was often a game going on at various locations up and down the street. There wasn't too much auto traffic in those days, especially above the tunnel mouth where tourists seldom ventured. In the early days, before the street was paved, there had been even less, they said. In fact, there is an old picture of Bingham Canyon that shows a horse peacefully napping in the middle of the street in front of the Bingham Hotel.

Even so, we were supposed to watch out for traffic as we batted our balls and hotfooted for home base, and I'm sure the town's drivers, too, tried to keep a sharp eye on us street-playing kids. Maybe it was more of a game of kids and traffic dodging each other than I remember, but I can't recall that we were ever ordered to stop playing in the street.

But it's a foregone conclusion that, if an accident had to happen it would happen to Betty Ann Contratto. One day when I was about seven we had a fast game going, just above the Knight Hotel, when a pickup came down the street. When headed down hill drivers had to use their brakes a lot, and their horns too, and the kids then took to the sidewalks until the vehicle had passed.

That day all the other players got out of the way in time, but I started too late, or didn't move fast enough. It was all over in seconds and I'll never know exactly what happened, but the pickup hit me and knocked me to the gravelly pavement. The frightened driver set his brakes, jumped out and picked me up. Blood was spurting all over both of us and I was screaming. Some of the kids ran in the hotel to get my mother.

"Get in and I'll take you to the hospital," the driver yelled at

Mom when she came running out. She leaped into the pickup seat and he put me on her lap and sped down to the Copper Hospital. There Dr. Frazier mopped the blood off my face and discovered that all I had was a deep cut on my chin. When he'd stitched me up I was as good as new, except for a couple of minor bruises—and the next day I was back on the street playing baseball.

Another of our favorite "games" was walking the high railroad trestles along the sides of the canyon above the street. We had great times, hopping from tie to tie, sometimes nearly one hundred feet above the ground. When an ore train came clanking along we jumped off the tracks at the last minute and hunkered up against the mountain while it went by, with the engineer leaning out of his window and yelling at us to get off the tracks before we got hurt, and to stay off. But as soon as the last car passed us we hopped back onto the ties again. I don't remember that anyone of us was ever hurt because of playing on the tracks.

The tramway was another of our play places. Its double set of tracks began at the upper end of Carr Fork, just above the Gemmell Club, and stood almost on end up the mountain side to the top, where the four-story mine office building towered into the sky. Two little box-like cars traveled on the tracks, pulled up and down by stout cables. The miners rode the tram up the hill to go to work, or to pick up their checks from the office on pay days, and down again when they came off their shifts in the mine.

The pay-master, the hiring boss and the mine manager all had offices in the building on top of the hill. The manager, Louis Buchman, was a short, stocky man who wore well-pressed khaki clothes and was always clean-shaven and very neat looking. He was always polite, and to my airy "Hi, Mr. Buchman," he invariably replied, "Good day, Betty Ann."

Tram passengers got into the little cars at either the top or the bottom of the hill and pushed either the "up" or "down" buttons and clanked off. One day a bunch of us kids got in the car at the bottom of the incline and pushed the "up" button. Yelling and laughing, we bumped up to the top, then pushed the "down" button and rode to the bottom.

It was such fun that, almost every day, we took a few rides in the tram cars. When the tram-master, who took a dim view of kids taking over his tram, saw that we weren't about to tire of it, he put a quick stop to it. He could operate the cars from a master switchboard in his office at the top and, after he had *asked* us to stop, explaining that we might have the car at the top when the mine workers or officials needed it at the bottom, or the other way around; and that we were apt to get hurt and maybe cost the company a lot of money, he had had to take sterner measures.

Asking us to stay off the tram hadn't kept us off, so one day when we had the car at the top the tram-master gave us a good scolding, then locked the car in position and made us walk down the mountain. We had a bad time of it, slipping, sliding and rolling to the bottom, around and through the rocks and gravel.

That cured us, my bunch anyway, and I never rode the tram again, even after I was older. But for a long time I missed the wonderful view from the top, where I could see the whole town of Bingham Canyon, scrunched into its Y shaped gash in the mountain, and many of the mine pits as well.

I had been told that, before my time and before they built the railroads and the tramway, the company had used huge iron ore buckets, swung on high cables, to carry the ore from the mines at the top of the mountain to the bins below, where it could be stored until hauled to the smelters at the mouth of the canyon. Some daring kids, they said, had used to ride the empty ore buckets as they went swinging and swaying along the cable back to the mines. I envied those long ago kids. If they had still had the ore buckets in my time I'm sure I would have ridden them, too, at least until I got into trouble and they ran me out of them.

Not everybody has a prime sledding hill right at his front door, but all of us in Bingham Canyon did, and we made full use of it, riding our sleds down the street almost every night all winter. Since the cars could barely get up the steep, snow-packed streets then, even with chains, there was little danger from traffic, especially at night.

After the first snow storm, as the street lights came on first one kid then another would hit the street, pulling a sled. Soon everybody except the very old and the toddlers would be out sleighing, two to a sled, all along the street.

I had my own sled, as did a lot of other kids, but some didn't. So when one of us came out, pulling a sled, a boy or girl who didn't have one would come running, get on, and away we'd go. We stopped our downward flight by dragging our feet or rolling off; then both of us grabbed the tow rope and pulled the sled up to the starting place again. One boy had a toboggan and we took turns piling onto that and riding it down the street aways. Some of the older kids often rode all the way down the whole length of the canyon; and that was great—except for the long pull back up hill to the starting point.

As we grew older Mom would, every now and then, let Don, Dottie and me invite our best friends in for refreshments after an evening of sleighing. Such times were very special, as she opened our seldom used parlor, built a fire in the big fireplace and let us roast wienies and marshmallows while she served us hot cocoa.

When we were about nine and eleven Mom bought Dottie and me each a bicycle. Some of our friends had them and we wanted to join the crowd on wheels. Mom, who had learned to ride a bicycle when she was a girl, undertook to teach us the art. She said it was easy, and no doubt it was, back there on the flat farm where she grew up. But on the steeply slanted street of Bingham Canyon it was different—and she hadn't been on a bike in years.

We took the new bicycles out on the sidewalk in front of the hotel and Mom got on mine. Before she could get control of her wheels they took off down the slope, wobbling like everything, and quickly dumped her. Though painfully bruised and scratched, she wasn't badly hurt; and she kept at it until she had mastered the machine again and taught us both to ride.

We used our bikes a good deal, either riding with our friends to get some place in a hurry. In either case riding *down* the street was fun, riding back *up* was work. But after I had the bike I didn't need to thumb rides with my taxi driver friends so often.

Mom had a friend, Mrs. Akins, who worked for the mining

company. She had a little office by the railroad tracks on the edge of the pit at the top of the canyon, where she pulled levers and pushed buttons, switching ore trains around down in the mine. Mrs. Akins had gone to work there when the United States got into the second World War and the mines had to employ many women to replace the men who'd gone into the service.

I had never been up there, so close to the big pit, and I'd been coaxing for a long time to go up to her office with her so I could see what it was like down in the mines. Mrs. Akins, another of my good friends, was an easygoing lady and willing to take me, but Mom was afraid I'd be a bother to her. I swore I wouldn't, but I'm afraid I was, when I finally got up there.

You see, she worked the four to midnight shift. By that time I was ten years old and I should have been getting over my phobia about being at home when night came—but I wasn't. When Mom finally gave in and said I could go, Mrs. Akins packed enough supper for both of us in her lunch bucket, then stopped for me and we walked across the street to the police station, just below the mouth of the tunnel.

Behind the station a flight of stairs one hundred steps high climbed the mountain side. We went up the stairs, then walked a short distance to the shack where she worked. It was exciting up there, where I could see across the mountain and look down into the enormous pit where the ore trains and trucks were shuttling back and forth. The tracks that carried the trains that ran down the mountain to the smelters were just outside the office door, and when a train came along I had to go inside while Mrs. Akins worked her switchboard.

The miners coming up the mountain to go to work, and those going off the afternoon shift, stopped to shoot the breeze a bit with Mrs. Akins, and to kid her about her new helper, me, and drink a cup of coffee. I enjoyed it all, the visiting, the passing trains, watching her work the switchboard. At supper time I thought it was neat, eating sandwiches and hardboiled eggs away up there above the town, and I was so happy just to be there.

And then the sun slid down behind the mountain and it began to get dark. I watched the stars come out, and the lights coming on, down in the mine and in the town—and I wanted to go home. Oh! How I wanted to go home.

From dark until midnight seemed an endless stretch of time for both Mrs. Akins and me. She coaxed me to look at the pictures in some magazines she had in her office. I tried to, and tried to go on watching the trains and whatever else was going on, but all I really wanted was to go home. I would have gone down that long stretch of stairs by myself to get to my home but Mrs. Akins wouldn't let me. So I passed the time by jumping up and running to the windows, and then to the door and back to my chair, then round again until I fairly drove my poor friend wild.

Midnight came at last, and with it Mrs. Akins' relief operator, and we went down the stairs and I ran across the street to the hotel and my own bed. I never again asked to go up to the office on the top of the mountain—and I'm sure Mrs. Akins wouldn't have taken me if I had.

The Gemmell Club at the upper end of Carr Fork was, for the most part, for men only. The Utah Copper Company had build it to supply recreational facilities for its employees, all men at the time, and had named it for Robert Gemmell, an engineer who had helped develop the mine in its beginning years. Women were invited to the club for special occasions, but until I was eleven I had never been inside it and knew only by hearsay what it was like. Jean, one of my best friends, and I used to walk up Carr and look at it. A long building, three stories high at its tallest part, it was partly built in the hill and looked big and secretive from outside in the street. I had often asked to go inside but my folks said it was no place for kids, especially girls, so all we could do was look at the outside and speculate on the mysteries within. One afternoon we walked up to the Gemmel Club and found the side door standing open. We knew the men who used the club went there only in the evening, for the most part anyway, so we tip-toed inside. There we could hear people talking upstairs, where I later learned the rest rooms were located; and from the brooms and mop buckets sitting around we concluded the cleaning people were at work.

From where we stood we could see into a reading room at the

front. It was furnished with big overstuffed chairs and tables full of magazines. Card tables were scattered around and there were stuffed animal heads on the walls and spittoons on the floor. It looked elegant and comfortable and very mannish. Through another door we could see a big room with gymnasium equipment scattered around, and a balcony and a stage. They had dances in that room every once in a while, and after I was grown I went to some of them.

Just inside the side entrance where we stood the stairway to the basement went down. There didn't seem to be anyone around, so we slipped down the steps and looked about. We could see a locker room and a two-lane bowling alley (where I later bowled a few times) and a pool room; and through a nearby door we could see into a room with a boxing ring in the middle. We went in for a better look.

Some boxing gloves were hanging on hooks nearby, and right away we decided to put them on and have a show. But first we went to a pop machine near the door, put in our dimes and got a bottle apiece. After a swig or two we put on the gloves and made a few passes at each other with the awkward, bumbling things. Then we scooped up our bottles and had another drink. It wasn't easy to handle the bottles with the gloves on but we managed. Jean finished her drink and put her bottle down. I still had mine to my lips when I turned around to face my partner; and Jean, all squared away to take a swing at me, let fly before she saw the bottle. The blow smashed the glass hard against my teeth and I screamed as the blood began to flow.

As I'd done so many times before, I went howling home to Mom again. She cleaned me up and took me to Dr. Inglesby, our dentist. Besides a cut and bruised mouth, I had a broken tooth—and I hollered some more when Dr. Inglesby made the repairs.

I always considered that ordeal my punishment for going to the men's club that I'd been told to stay away from, and I had no desire to go back until I was grown, when I went there once in awhile to dances, or to basketball games and bowling matches.

Later on that same year another of my best friends, Lucy, and I decided to learn to smoke cigarettes, the real thing. We had been practicing for some time with bobby pins, holding them daintily between our first and second fingers and putting them into our mouths and puffing, then removing them gracefully, with our pinky fingers held just so. We criticized each other and made improvements (worthy a far better cause) in our technique until we were agreed that we had the hang of it very well.

Our mothers smoked, so it was easy for us to slip a cigarette or two into our pockets in preparation for the big day. Before long I found that Mom was going out for awhile, so I called Lucy and told her to come over, that now was our chance to try the real thing in our bathroom. Lucy hurried over and, all excited, we locked ourselves in the bathroom and lit up.

For a little while, a very little while, it was fun. We puffed, and choked on the smoke, and puffed some more. Then, just as it seemed that we were really getting onto it, we got sick. We both turned green and our stomachs turned over and we heaved up everything we'd eaten for a week. Weak as a pair of wet noodles, we cleaned up all the evidence of our adventure and SWORE OFF SMOKING FOR GOOD.

Our fervent resolution lasted until we felt normal again, and for a few months afterward. Then brother Don's current girl invited us to stay all night with her at her home in Salt Lake. By then I had stayed all night once in awhile with either Jean or Lucy, there in Bingham Canyon, and had found that I *could* actually sleep in a bed other than my own.

Don's friend smoked and, that night in her room, we begged her to show us how. Some of the other girls in the seventh grade were smoking on the sly and we felt that we just had to learn, too. Agnes was willing. "Take deep breaths," she instructed us, "then blow out slow through your noses." We did, and it made us sick and dizzy at first, but not nearly as sick as we had been the time before. We kept at it that night, and after we'd finished a couple of cigarettes apiece we found that it didn't bother us much any more. I smoked for years after that, sneaking them out of Mom's supply and doing it on the sly for as long as I was at home, and then on my own until I quit.

And finally there was the battle of the clotheslines, once a year on Hollowe'en night. In those days Monday was wash day in Bingham Canyon, when the whole town's clothes hung out in full view all up and down the street. There was no hiding the family wash in the back yard in our town; for, with no back yards and all the houses stacked up the way they were, the clothes lines ran from the front of each dwelling to telephone poles, trees, other houses, anything solid enough to hold up a line of wet wash. Some lines ran from a house on one side of the street to another house on the other side. Most of the lines worked on pulleys and the housewife stood on her porch, above the street, and pulled the line to her as she pinned on the wash.

The lines had many uses. Our Spanish neighbor, across the alley above Henry's house, used hers to hang her rugs on for their regular Saturday beating. I can see her yet, a stocky lady with her heavy black hair protected by a gay scarf, beating her rugs with might and main while she sang at the top of her voice, a lively Spanish melody to which she kept time with her thumping and whacking while the dust flew to the four winds.

Throughout the year—until Hallowe'en—the clothes lines were subject only to the hazards of wind and weather; but on that night the town kids tried to make sure that every single one came down before morning. Many of the owners tried to see that they didn't, and so the annual battle raged, with the kids usually the winners.

As soon as I was old enough I raced up and down the street with the kid pack, helping make war on the clothes lines. We slipped in, under cover of darkness, and cut the lines that didn't seem to be protected, then dashed away. After it came time for the girls to go home to bed, the boys usually managed to snip most of the remaining lines, and then turned their attention to the privies.

Many families still had outdoor bathrooms and the boys did their best to overturn every last one of them before morning. Some of the owners tried to prevent that, too, and one was Orange Baker of Carr Fork. Tired of setting his outhouse up again after every Hallowe'en, one night he retired to the little building with his shotgun, determined to wait out the siege. But the raiders found out he had forted up inside it, so instead of pushing it over they roped it and, from a safe distance, pulled it over with the defender trapped inside. Mr. Baker's daughter, Ivy, grew up to become Ivy Baker Priest, treasurer of the United States while D. D. Eisenhower was president.

Chapter Seven

Growing Up

Except for the small change and spending money the Bingham Canyon kids had for ice cream, candy and pop, everybody charged everything in our town. My folks had charge accounts at the Bingham Merc, both drugstores, the butcher shop, the garage, just about everywhere in town. From the time I was about five I had been given leave to use the accounts and charge anything I needed at the drugstores and the Bingham Merc. That saved Dad and Mom the bother of dishing out nickels and dimes for candy, cones and other little necessities.

For quite awhile the arrangement worked fine, for my needs were modest, and anyway I usually had my own spending money, due to my summertime ore business and the generosity of my grandparents and the miners. During school terms, however, my income fell off drastically as the tourist season was over and I was usually in school on pay days. Also, as I grew older, my needs ballooned.

I am naturally of a generous nature, and I had lots of friends. The year I started the fifth grade it was unusually warm in the fall. So, after school in the afternoons, I began taking a gang of my schoolmates, five or six at a time, to the Number One Evans Drugstore and treating them to cones, sundaes, banana splits, anything cooling that the fountain could supply.

"Just order anything you want," I'd tell the kids. They did, and I felt like a big shot, as I seemed to be the only kid in the fifth grade who was privileged to be a big spender. After I'd treated my ever-growing group of friends a number of times, Mr. Evans began cautioning me to take it easy—but I would reply airily, "Oh, it's all right. My Mom don't care how much I spend here." Then Mr. Evans would shake his head and fill the orders, and I'd go on feeling like a big shot.

Pretty soon some of my girl friends and I became interested in perfume. The drugstore stocked some fancy little bottles of perfume with high sounding names like Djer-Kiss, June Rose and Khiva Bouquet, and we'd ask to look at them, then pull the stoppers and take a sniff all around. I was enjoying my role of "big spender" so much by then that I took the bottle we agreed had the best smell, told the clerk to "charge it" and passed the vial around for everyone to put a dab on herself until it was all gone.

This became a regular routine. We'd watch the perfume counter for new shipments and each time they came in I'd ask to see the new brands—and end up buying a bottle and dousing all of us with it.

All went well for a few weeks, and then my career as a dispenser of largesse came to a sudden end. One afternoon I lined my gang up at the soda fountain, only to have Mr. Evans tell me my account had been closed and he couldn't serve us unless I had the cash to pay.

Of course I didn't have the cash, but, undaunted, I led the way outside and said, "Come on, kids, we'll go down to the other store." Away we went down the hill to the Evans Number Two, only to be told the same thing at the soda fountain there. I was angry and deeply humiliated, but there was nothing I could do—except to go home and ask Mom *why*?

"Ann," she said, "when Dad paid the bill yesterday, your share of it was over $60, and we don't have *that* kind of money."

I couldn't believe it! Cones were a nickel, sodas and sundaes a dime, even the fanciest banana split was no more than a quarter. Then Mom explained that it was the perfume that had caused all the trouble, especially after I started charging the more expensive kinds, three or four dollars a bottle, and anyway, she didn't think ten- and eleven-year-olds needed perfume.

I had charge account trouble again when I was in the seventh grade, this time at the Bingham Merc. The store stocked extensive lines of dresses, shoes, hose and accessories of all kinds; and that was the year I became clothes conscious and developed a desire to impress the kids in my class with my garb—the girls, of course, and two or three of the best looking boys.

Until then boys had been fun to play games with and to run the streets with, always in a group or gang. But that year I began noticing boys as individuals; the best looking, the most comical, the most popular. The ones who attracted me most didn't seem to pay much attention to me—and I thought some fancy new clothes might improve the situation.

So I went to the clothing department at the Bingham Merc and tried on dresses until I found the one I liked the best. I charged it of course, and then decided I needed new shoes to wear with it. I charged those too, and Mom didn't say anything when I wore the new outfit to school the next day. Probably she was so busy she didn't even notice, or maybe she thought it was time I had some new things and was glad I had taken care of it.

After a few days I tired of that dress, so I went back to the store and bought another one. I bought half a dozen new dresses in the next few weeks, and bought hair ribbons as well, and new scarves and mittens as the weather grew colder, and anything else I took a fancy to. It was all so easy.

And then Dad went in and paid the Merc bill. It was so much bigger than it had ever been before that he took it home and "analyzed" it. It was soon plain that I was the culprit—and I was cut off again. From then on I had to present Mr. Adderley a note showing what I was supposed to buy that trip, and the maximum price allowed.

Perhaps that clothes buying spree of mine first gave Dad the idea about sending me away to a girls' school where the students wore only uniforms. That, and the fact that I was becoming "boy crazy," and he knew I wouldn't be seeing many boys at a girls' school.

Looking back on it now, it's hard to believe that I could ever have been so silly. It must be that going "nuts" over boys is an invisible thing like a virus that attacks most girls about the time they reach their teens; anyway Lucy and I had it bad, the spring that marked the end of our first year in Copperton high school.

We did everything together, Lucy and I, so we both got a crush on a senior boy. He was terribly good looking, or so we thought, and just "super" in every way and we lost our heads over him. The fact that he had a steady girl friend, another senior, made no difference to us. We used to take turns calling him up at his home, then hanging up when he answered the phone, our heads swimming with delight just to have heard his voice one more time. We tagged him around at school, staring at him moon-eyed, hoping that some day he'd notice us.

We finally screwed up our courage enough to ask him if he would, please, just kiss our hands. He stared at us in surprise for a minute, then laughed and grabbed us, Lucy first and then me, and kissed us on our cheeks. We went off in a daze—and pledged each other that we wouldn't wash our faces for days. For me that was a big sacrifice on the altar of love, the way I liked bathing all over, two or three times a day if I could manage it.

Naturally our Light of Love's steady girl friend took a dim view of Lucy and me and our silly tricks. After the kissing episode she cornered us on the bus on the way home and told us to stop hanging around Jack or she'd do something about it. "Just go off and grow up," she snapped at us in parting.

We didn't care for her attitude but she didn't really scare us. It would take more than an angry girl friend to chill our love for our idol. However, school was out a short time later and that did it. When we no longer saw the object of our devotion every day we soon forgot him.

Some of the Bingham Canyon boys our age acquired old cars that summer and our gang took to wheels, instead of covering the town on foot as we had before. We'd fill an old single-seater coupe, or a touring model Ford or Chevy brim-full of bodies and putt-putt around, free and airy and independent.

One day I was at Lucy's house when one of our friends and two or three of his pals drove up and, for some reason or other, *backed* into the driveway in front of the garage; for Lucy's dad had a nice car, and a little garage at the side of his house to keep it in. Fortunately, he was gone with the car that day.

The boys got out of the car and Lucy and I got in. We kidded around awhile, and then I told the owner of the jalopy that we knew how to drive and were going to take his heap for a spin. He said, "Sure, go ahead," and cranked the old motor for us. So there we were, all set to take off, except that we *didn't* know how to drive, in more than a vague and general way, that is. But we couldn't back out then, it had gone too far for that.

I was under the wheel and, leaning over, I whispered to Lucy that if she'd shift the gears I'd steer. Lucy was game and, reaching across me, she gave the shift lever a hefty yank. We instantly dashed backward at high speed and crashed through the garage doors behind us. I got the car stopped, somehow, just before we barreled right on through the back end of the little building and into the mountain behind it.

Chapter Eight

Galena Days
and Other Celebrations

Because of the many nationalities in Bingham Canyon there were so many holidays and festivals that celebrations seemed to be going on the year around. The Greeks had their Name Days and other festivals, as did the Chinese, the Germans, the Ser-bian-Austrians, the Swedes, the Spanish, the Italians, and other smaller groups.

The nationals of each country celebrated in their own way, and members of other nationalities, unless specifically invited, could only look on from the outside. The Germans had their special Christmas festival, lasting several days; so did the Swedes and Norwegians. The Serbian-Austrians roasted whole pigs out of doors for their Christmas, which started on January 7 and lasted three days. Their Christmas started on that date because of the Gregorian Calendar.

The Chinese prepared their traditional dishes for their National New Year, and celebrated with firecrackers all day long. Music, dancing and feasting kept things lively at the Spanish festivals, and the same was true of Italian special days.

My family took part in Italian Day, which belonged to all of

Some of the clotheslines spanning Bingham Canyon's street. Courtesy Utah State Historical Society.

The mine passenger tram up the mountainside to the Company offices at the top.

The high ore train trestle that spanned the street. Bingham Merc in foreground. Courtesy Utah State Historical Society.

Tourist cars waiting for the green light to enter the tunnel and drive through to the copperfield side to see the "Richest Hole on Earth."

Photographed about 1909, the Bingham Mercantile Company was constructed in 1907 and torn down in 1960. Courtesy Utah State Historical Society Photographic Collection.

us who were Italian either by birth or marriage. We celebrated with a huge picnic, held up in Butterfield Canyon on the outskirts of town. The men built big campfires and cooked kettles of palenta and roasted a pig and many chickens. The women made the salads, set the long tables, fixed gallons of cold drinks and looked after the babies. When everything else was ready the men began frying hamburgers and roasting hot dogs.

At noon we ate all we could hold of the delicious and highly seasoned food, then collapsed for a short siesta. As soon as we were able to move again, the older men brought out their accordians and made music the rest of the day, while the rest of us sang and danced the hours away, the kids as well as the grownups. During the forenoons, while the older folks were busy with the food, Dottie and I and the other Italian kids raced and screamed and played games. Don, several years older, and other teenage couples found secluded spots and carried on their courting, an important business that seemed awfully funny to us young fry.

After a few Italian Days in Butterfield Canyon, our elders moved the celebration to Lagoon, a big amusement park near Salt Lake City. After that we took our picnic foods already prepared and there were no more big campfires and cookouts; but the carnival rides were more fun for the young folks and we still had great times.

In addition to the special days of all the different colonies in the Canyon, we had two holidays in which *everybody* took part— the Fourth of July and Galena Days. Those holidays were exciting and fun, but, because of my heritage, Italian Day was *mine* and very special to me; and I suppose the people of the other nationalities felt the same way about *their* days.

I was five on the first Fourth that stands out in my memory. Mom had made Dottie and me white satin blouses and red satin skirts, held together with blue satin sashes around our middles. That morning she cleaned us up and dressed us in our pretty outfits, then ordered us to be careful and not get dirty or mussed up while she got herself ready.

For once I minded, sitting primly on my chair and scarcely moving, although I was wild to get out on the street where firecrackers were popping like mad and the celebration was getting livlier by the minute. So Dottie was the one who got into trouble that time. While Mom's back was turned she helped herself to the lipstick, mascara and rouge on the dressing table and smeared makeup on her satin outfit as well as on her face. Then I, Betty Ann, for once was able to run and tell Mom to come see how Dottie had messed herself up, and to point out how nice *I* still looked. Poor Mom. She spanked Dottie, undressed her and washed and pressed her clothes, then dressed her up again. We were late in joining the action on the street, but it was almost worth it—just once being the sister who hadn't gotten into trouble.

Besides all the noise and happy confusion of the day, there were contests and races for everybody, and a parade and food stands and fireworks. There were races for even the little kids like me and everyone who ran got a prize, a quarter apiece, all around.

But there were some people in the town who objected to the terrific noise of the exploding firecrackers that went on from before dawn until long after dark. There had been some injuries from them, too, and one boy had had his thumb blown off, so the town council passed a law and the word went out—no more firecrackers on the Fourth of July. Sparklers were all right, and families could have all the fireworks they wanted, except firecrackers.

Naturally the kids, including me, felt cheated. Even so there were some firecrackers around that day, and I got hold of one. Of course our town policemen were on the street all day, watching to see that there were no violations. All the Bingham Canyon kids knew the police by name, and the police knew all the kids and there was a friendly relationship between us. The officers seldom had to get tough with any of us; for we knew they were looking after us and we liked and respected them. Besides, my father had been appointed Chief of Police a few months earlier and I was proud of that, and probably felt that it gave me a little extra immunity where the police were concerned.

Anyway, I had a firecracker and I intended to light it, even though I knew I wasn't supposed to. Just then one of the officers came along and spotted my cracker and my match before I could hide them. I don't remember, now, which policeman it was, but when he saw what I was about to do he said, "Betty Ann, you're not supposed to light a firecracker." But I was sure he wouldn't do anything to me if I did, so quick as a wink I lighted the cracker and threw it into the street.

I saw instantly that I'd made a mistake, but it was a lot worse than I'd expected. My firecracker had no sooner gone off than the officer took me by the arm and started marching me down toward the jail. That really scared me and I began to tell him how sorry I was that I'd broken the law, and to beg him to let me go. But he wouldn't. He took me all the way to the jail, and then inside it, and steered me toward a cell. I couldn't believe that he would actually put me in that cell, but he did, and locked the door.

Then he went away and left me. There was no one else in the jail, just me, locked in and all alone. At first I was stunned. The fact that my dad was Chief of Police hadn't helped. I was actually in jail and I had no idea how long I'd be there. What if I had to spend the NIGHT there? I began to bawl. I really howled, and it seemed to me I kept it up for hours. Anyway I was weak as a wet rag when the officer came back and turned me loose. Probably I had been in that cell no more than fifteen minutes but it was long enough to teach me the hardest lesson of my life. When the policeman asked me if I was ready to behave, I said "yes," and I meant it. To this day I've never lighted another firecracker—and neither have I ever knowingly broken a law of the land.

Galena Days were about the same as the Fourth of July and Italian Day, only they lasted *three days and nights* and everybody in town, including visitors, celebrated for as long as they could keep up the pace, then rested a bit and joined in again.

The Junior Chamber of Commerce started Galena Days (so-called for the Galena mine where ore was first discovered in 1863 at the highest point of the canyon) by holding the first celebration in 1939, the year I was seven. Their purpose was to honor the old-timers who had started the town more than half a century earlier, and to give the present population an idea of what life had been like in the canyon all those years ago. All the different nationalities dressed in old fashioned clothes, with lots of long skirts and sunbonnets, and a big parade wound its way up the canyon each forenoon.

I remember some of the men, in boots and neckerchiefs, leading little mules or burros bearing packs, just like they used to have in the early prospecting days. The miners were mixed in with beautiful floats, and with clowns doing their stunts. Bands marched and played and it was all so lively and gay. Before long Galena Days parades were acclaimed the best anywhere around, even better than Salt Lake City could put on.

During the celebration all the bars and gambling places were open to everybody, even the kids. During those three days we could go in the saloons and right up to the bar and order our drinks just like the grownups. Of course they served us only pop or lemonade, but it was exciting for us because we were not allowed in such places any other time of the year.

Naturally I went into all of the places. The gambling tables fascinated me and I watched the men playing and betting their money until I had a working idea of how it was done. At one place I had a dollar, so I laid it on a square just as the dealer rolled the dice. Of course I lost my dollar, and when the dealer scraped it in with the other losers' money I let out a squawl.

Until then I hadn't been noticed in the crowd around the table, but when the dealer heard my howl and took a look at me he was quite upset. Even though everything was open to everybody, it was still against the law for minors to play the table or to gamble, and I could have gotten that dealer into trouble. He gave me back my dollar and scooted me out of his place in a hurry.

There were slot machines, too, scores of them, probably brought in from Nevada and set up in the street. Kids weren't supposed to play those either, but I did—and I lost every time because, after I'd dropped in my money and pulled the lever, I ran away, afraid to stay long enough to see if I'd won anything. Big traveling carnival companies made our annual celebration and set up in the street for the whole three days. I rode everything, and played the games of chance, which were not illegal for kids, until I ran out of money. Then I'd hunt up Mom or Dad, or Grandpa or Grandma, and get some more.

All up and down the street, in every otherwise unoccupied

nook or corner, there were tables full of food. Each one of Bingham Canyon's many ethnic groups had its own specialty for sale. The Italians, the Spanish, Mexican, Chinese, Greek, Japanese, German, and Swedish people had their tables loaded with delicacies; the Americans had their hot dog, hamburger and pop stands, and we always had watermelons by the truckload, hauled in from the gardens in the valley below. I ate all I could hold of everything, and especially the *hot* varieties.

As far back as I can remember I have loved the hottest, spiciest foods anyone could put together. Even on ordinary days, when nothing special was going on, I often went to the Mexican restaurant up the street and ordered their biggest chili, with lots of hot sauce, and ate every spoonful. Even the Mexican and Spanish people were surprised that I could do it—let alone *like* it.

There were contests every day of the Galena celebration, all kinds, for the kids and everybody. The miners had mucking and panning contests, to see who among them could still do the best, or fastest, job. For the kids there were races every day: foot races, sack races, three-legged races. In one contest we all took off our shoes and some grownups tied the shoestrings together and threw them into a common pile. At the word "Go" we tore into the pile, looking for our shoes. The kid who could find his own shoes, untie the laces and get his footgear on again, and laced and tied, won the race.

One year I won the kids' pie eating contest, and the three dollar cash prize. Eight of us entered that race, so they lined eight cherry pies up on a table and stood a kid in front of each pie. Then they tied our hands behind our backs and hollered "Go."

I probably had as much pie *on* my face as inside it—but my pan was empty first. I had pie up my nose and in my hair and dripping off my chin, but I was the winner. I grabbed my three silver dollars—and then ran home and took a bath.

At night everybody danced in the streets. Some hardy souls would still be dancing at dawn, while the rest of the crowd was catching a little rest and sleep before the next day's fun began in earnest. On the morning after the first full day and night of the first Galena Days celebration, Mr. Quinn, one of our most prominent and popular businessmen, and two of his friends went up and down the street hunting for breakfast. Long lines of people waited in front of every cafe and restaurant in town, and while they stood in one of the lines one of the men said he knew of a place in San Francisco that served great breakfasts. The three of them immediately decided to go there for their pancakes. Piling into a car, they drove to Salt Lake, bought plane tickets and flew to California for breakfast.

On the first day of every Galena celebration it was the same: all of the kids in Bingham Canyon, Carr Fork, Freeman Gulch, Highland Boy, Copperfield and Lead Mine were out by daylight. By ones, twos or threes they hit the street, gathered in herds and raced up and down the canyon, everyone shouting greetings and messages to everyone else. The groups were constantly changing, getting larger or smaller as kids dropped out of one group to join another, or new kids arrived to join in and run, laughing and yelling, from one fun place to another, all so carefree and happy. When any of us played out completely, or some of our mothers collared us, we'd go home to rest and nap a little while, then run back and get into the swing of things again. Day and night, for the whole three days and nights, it was like that. Most of us would never again know such happy times.

There was one other celebration I'll never forget, one that happened one time and one time only—Armistice Day, 1945. The one I remember was really the second one, the end of the second great world war. I was only thirteen when it ended but I had had a pretty good idea of what it was all about, and what it had meant to Bingham Canyon.

Almost every family in our town had had someone in the war, many of them overseas in the thick of the fighting, two of Dad's brothers among them. They both came home again, but the fifteen home town boys who gave their lives for their country represented most of our many nationalities: English, German, Greek, Swedish, Italian, Jewish, Serbian.

My father had served as president of the Bingham Canyon chapter of the Victory Flag Society, organized by Carl Zahos (Chicago Charlie) and untiring in its support of the United States during the great conflict. So it was a big day when news

65

of the war's end was flashed to Bingham Canyon. Everybody who wasn't sick abed was out on the street, singing, crying, shouting, dancing, honking their car horns, heading for the bars. The celebration went on far into the night, and the release of fear, tension and anger that had gripped the town since the war had been declared was an almost visible thing.

Leaving Home

My happy days came to an end with my fourteenth summer, the fall that I was ready for eighth grade. As I've mentioned before, my father was a Roman Catholic and my mother a Mormon. When I was small I was baptized in the Mormon church and, when we occasionally attended church, we went to services there with Mom. When I grew older Mom would get me ready for Sunday School and church and send me by myself, but I usually went to Lucy's house instead and stayed until the time to show up at home again.

Mom had told Dottie and me about God, and that He loved and watched over us, but I knew next to nothing about the Bible or any meaningful kind of worship and, on the principle that you don't miss what you haven't had, I was quite satisfied that way. When, that summer, my parents made arrangements to send me to a Catholic girls school over the state border in Idaho I didn't want to go. In fact, I was determined not to go.

For one thing it would mean that, for months at a time, I wouldn't be home at night, sleeping in my own bed. For another, I'd have to go away and leave all my friends, the kids and the townspeople that I loved. I'd even have to leave Dottie—and for the first time I realized that I'd miss *her*, too.

But no matter how I reasoned, begged and pleaded, I couldn't talk my folks out of it. So, in September, off I went to school; and it was much worse than anything I'd even imagined. Everything at the school was so different from my carefree life at home in bingham Canyon. At school I lived by rules and regulations from morning until night, like in the army. No more doing as I pleased, when I pleased, except on pain of punishment. I don't mean that it was *all* bad, and I think the girls who had been used to more discipline didn't mind it at all, or even liked it. It was just that I was so impulsive, so used to acting before I thought, and at the school such behavior couldn't be tolerated. As time went on I became really fond of the Mother Superior and of one or two of the nuns, and I made some good friends among the girls I met there. Looking back on it now I know that, in spite of the rigid discipline, I had some good times there.

There were about one hundred girls in the school, ranging from first graders up through high school. The Sisters were equally strict with all of us, right from the first day, to the very end. They put us in uniforms as soon as we arrived—navy blue dresses with long sleeves and white collars, long nylon hose and oxford shoes. That was bad enough, but the fact that the uniforms were made of wool, and that we had to wear the hot, itchy things in the fall and spring, while the weather was still very warm, made them a nightmare.

We were divided into groups of seven girls of approximately the same age for meals. Each group sat at a table for eight, with a Sister in the head chair. Discipline began at breakfast with special emphasis on table manners. The food was good enough but there were a few things I didn't like and had never eaten at home. The Sister served our plates with even portions for everybody and we were expected to eat every bite.

The first time I left a vegetable untouched on my plate the Sister asked me why, and when I told her I didn't like it she quickly made me eat it, and then a second helping as well. Liver was one food I couldn't stand. The first time we had it I explained to her that it made me sick. Her reply was to make me eat a double portion. I ate it as fast as I could, swallowed the last bite, then excused myself and ran out and threw up. With a rule like that I soon learned to eat everything and keep still about the ones I didn't like.

We were punished if we forgot to say please and thank you, and for talking with food in our mouths. We had to hold our knives and forks just so and eat daintily and observe what seemed to me to be an endless list of "dos" and "don'ts." Neither did I like having to get up early every morning and go to chapel before breakfast. The first morning I was scared and uncertain as we took our places in the chapel, so I whispered to the Sister in charge of my group and asked her what I was supposed to do. Just do as the others do, she told me. So I did; I knelt when they did and stood up when they did and all seemed to be going well.

Then, when we came to the Communion part and the other girls went up to the front to take the wine and wafer, I did the same thing—and didn't know I had made a serious mistake until the Sister caught hold of my sleeve and pulled me firmly out of the line. She told me that I had just done a very wicked thing because, since I had never studied the catechism, nor been confirmed, I was not really a Catholic and had no right to take communion. After that, although I still did all the other things, I stayed in my seat while the other girls took communion.

Mom and Dad had told me a little about communion, but I didn't know the religious significance of the word, so had had no idea that I was out of line when I was carefully trying to "do as the others do." And I suppose that poor Sister just couldn't comprehend how anyone could be as ignorant and mixed up about religious matters as I was. I didn't know, either, but I was sure finding out the hard way.

The dorms held six girls each, with a sister in charge of each one. Our narrow beds, or cots, were lined up down the long room, with the Sister's bed in a curtained alcove at the far end of the room. Some of the girls in my dorm quite often received packages of candy, cookies and other goodies from home. Mom sent me packages, too, and whenever one of us had one we all gathered on the bed of the lucky girl and stuffed ourselves.

This was also against the rules, of course, so we had to pick our times to enjoy our treats. The best time seemed to be while the nuns were at prayers; but we didn't always calculate right, in which case we were caught and punished. Some times we had to hold our little picnics at night, and when that happened we waited until we were sure our Sister supervisor was asleep behind her curtain. Then we'd slip out of our beds and slither across the floor on our stomachs to the right bed. We'd do all right for a little while—until someone giggled and waked the Sister, and then we'd be in trouble again.

In my dorm we all got to wondering a lot about the nuns, living in their own mysterious world, and what went on in their private lives during the hours when we didn't see them. We were especially curious as to whether they shaved their heads or not. We had heard that they did, but they all wore their wimples whenever we saw them and we couldn't tell if they had any hair or not.

We finally figured that they surely didn't *sleep* in their veils, so the time to find out would be when our Sister was asleep. My dorm mates had soon learned that I was the most daring of anyone in our group, so they dared me to take a look at Sister Ann when she was asleep. They didn't have to urge me very much, for I wanted so much to know if she was baldheaded that it fairly made my teeth ache.

On the night we decided to find out we waited until everything had been quiet for quite awhile and we were dead sure the Sister was asleep. Then I slithered out of my bed and down the long room on my stomach. We girls slithered on our stomachs so much at school that it was a wonder we didn't have calluses on them. I thought I was doing real well and not making a sound, but when I finally reached Sister Ann's alcove, soundlessly pulled the curtain back and looked up—there she was, still in her wimple, and staring down at me in the dim light of her little night lamp.

She sternly ordered me to get back into bed and stay there, and promised that she would "take care of me" in the morning. So I had that to worry about the rest of the night.

One frequent punishment was being assigned to shampoo the little girls' hair. Some of the girls despised having to do that but I didn't mind at all. I have always loved little kids and being with those little girls while I washed their hair and prettied them up was fun. The other most used punishment was having to wash stacks of dirty dishes. Even that wasn't too bad for me, though most of the girls hated it, because I've never minded hard work. I just washed and dried as fast as I could and was through in no time. Maybe that was one reason why I was punished so often—I turned out a lot of free labor for that school in my time there.

The school was a big four-story brick building with long, steep stairways between the floors. A wide, glistening bannister bordered the outside of each flight and there was a big garbage can at the foot of each stairway, where waste paper and other debris from the school rooms and dorms was collected. Of course I slid down the bannister at every opportunity, when there wasn't a Sister in sight. For awhile I got away with it, but one time I missed seeing the nun, or else she walked in from somewhere after I had checked the area, for when I came whizzing down the bannister she stepped out in front of me and, just before I landed, snatched a garbage can and swung it around onto my landing spot. I plopped into it pretty hard—and was in trouble again.

There was a big gymnasium where we played volley ball, soft ball and the like. The floor was kept waxed and polished until we could see our faces in it and I loved to slide across it in my stockinged feet. One day I had a little girl sit on a chair while I slid her all over the room on the freshly waxed surface. We raced and whirled and had a great time—until I finally noticed the awful scratches we'd made all over the floor. Trouble again!

At the school the only time we ever got to see any boys was on the Saturday afternoons when we went to the picture show downtown, which was within walking distance of the school. However, the punishment for those of us who broke the rules most often was to take away our movie privileges, and I was in trouble so much that I almost *never* got to go to the shows, and that was a real punishment as far as I was concerned.

I had always had the Bingham Canyon boys for friends and playmates and I had long been addicted to movies, so having to stay at the school on Saturday afternoons, week after week, was really hard on me, especially now that I had begun to take a different kind of interest in boys. And most of the time I hadn't meant to be bad, or to break a rule; it was just that there were so many of them and I was so impulsive, acting without thinking, that I was in trouble before I knew what I'd done that I shouldn't. Maybe I was a little unlucky, too, getting caught doing things that more careful girls got away with.

Finally I grew so desperate that, when a letter came from Mom one day, I read it, then hurried to the Mother Superior. Now I dearly loved that good lady and hated to lie to her, but I told her my mother was awfully sick and needed me at home. Actually everything was fine in Bingham Canyon, but I was hoping they'd put me right on the bus and send me home. Instead, Mother Superior went to the phone and called Mom.

The result of that was that Mom and Dad drove to the school and had a talk with me. They were nice about it and even took me downtown for supper—but they let me know that it must *never* happen again, and that another lie would land me in real trouble. So I didn't get to go home until Christmas vacation.

It was great to be at home again, where I could shed the picky manners I had to observe at school, pass up the things I didn't like to eat, go to the movies and have an all around good time. Every chance I had I put up a good case for not going back to school, but in spite of all my arguments, tears and protests, I had to go back at the end of the holidays.

Notwithstanding my carelessness and all my infractions of the rules, two of the nuns liked me and let my folks know it. In return Dad and Mom invited them to visit us in Bingham Canyon that summer. Dad arranged for a picnic while they were with us and we all went up to Butterfield Canyon and picked out a shady table and benches. Dad and Mom loaded the table with their best picnic treats and we all sat down to eat. Dad had seated the nuns on the best bench, which was on the downhill side of the table, and when he asked Sister Jean to say the blessing we all bowed our heads. At that instant Sister's bench tipped over on the sloping ground and we all looked up in time to see her going head-over-heels backward down the hill, with her long habit up over her head and her feet in the air. Poor Sister Jean. She and the other nun were both too mortified to enjoy the rest of the picnic.

I remembered to mind my manners while the Sisters were with us, but after they left I happily reverted to my usual unrefined state. That was one of the good things about vacations from school—from the moment I arrived home I could drop my society manners and be myself.

I was fifteen that summer and determined to learn to drive a car. Automobiles had always fascinated me—but it was a wonder that I ever lived long enough to grow up and learn to drive one. Several years earlier, when I was only five or six, I had climbed into a car parked halfway up the street between my home and the top of the mountain. The emergency brake was on, of course, to keep it from rolling down the hill. I sat under the wheel and 'steered" for awhile, then I began pushing and pulling things and finally got the brake off. Away I went.

The retainer wall that held the mountain slope in place at the mouth of the tunnel was several hundred yards below me. A high, thick cement barracade, it was located just off to the side of the street and I was headed straight for it at a high rate of speed. The head-on crash would probably have splattered me all over that wall—if a man on the street hadn't seen me, raced out and bull-dogged that car. He stopped it only inches short of the barracade.

However I did learn to drive and could handle a car pretty well before that vacation was over. Jake, one of the men who lived at our hotel, had an old Model A Ford and one of Mom's sisters, Aunt Dez, was visiting us. Although several years older than I, she was always ready for a prank or anything that sounded like fun. One day we decided that, if Jake would let us borrow his car, we'd go for a ride. At that stage I was still only a "learner" and was surprised that Jake let me take his car, but he said "Sure," and fished the crank out from under the seat. We got in, with me under the wheel, and he cranked it up.

"Now remember," he said, "you can't stop anyplace or the engine will quit and you can't crank it up again. Just keep going 'til you get back."

Waving, and yelling "So long, Jake," we drove away, leaving

him standing there with the crank in his hand. Before we'd gone far Aunt Dez said we should stop at Darcy's and get a hamburger apiece. "We don't dare stop," I reminded her. ""If we do the engine will die and we can't start it again." She said, "Never mind, just drive by Darcy's as slow as you can."

Darcy's hamburger stand was right up against the pavement, like all the other buildings on the street, but it had a narrow driveway that circled it and led back onto the street again. So I drove as slowly as I dared and Aunt Dez shouted to Mrs. Darcy to fry us two hamburgers right quick. We drove on around and went by again. "Put onions and pickles on 'em," she yelled. When we came around the third time Mrs. Darcy was at the edge of the street with our hamburgers in napkins. Aunt Dez grabbed them and dropped the money in the lady's hand as we drove on.

I had some real honest-to-goodness dates that summer, too. Some Dad and Mom knew about and some they didn't. When I suspected that there might be a question as to whether or not they'd let me go, I just told the boy who had asked me that I'd meet him at a designated time and place, then went to my room and got ready. When it was about time to meet my date I simply climbed through the air shaft windows into Don's room and slipped out his door into the alley. It really seemed more fun to go on a clandestine date than on one the folks knew about.

That summer, and the next, I went a few times to the dances at the American Legion Civic Center. They were the big dances of the town, with paid music and all that, but I wasn't supposed to go to them. For one thing the crowd that went there was an older group than mine; for another, the Army brought bus loads of soldiers over from the Kerns Army Base to the dances. Because of the soldiers our parents said they were no place for fifteen- and sixteen-year-olds, and so forbid us to go.

Every now and then, though, I'd go with some of the kids my age, "just to watch a little while," but as soon as we got inside I'd be asked to dance. So I danced, but I didn't really enjoy it because I knew there was a good chance I'd be caught. As Chief of Police, Dad kept a pretty close watch on those dances, and every other kind of public entertainment in town, so I spent most of my time on the dance floor watching for my father to show up. If he did I knew I'd be in big trouble and, after getting away with one or two dances, I went on to safer localities.

And then vacation was over and, in spite of all my arguments and tears, I had to go back to school again.

Chapter Ten

More Growing Up

I didn't get into trouble quite so much at school, that year, so I got to go to the movies a couple of times that fall. Some of the senior girls usually had movie privileges every Saturday and the Mother Superior put them in charge of us freshmen and sophomores, with strict orders to us to obey them and behave ourselves.

That would have worked all right except that, the last time any of us got to go, the seniors had other plans for the afternoon. When we reached the theater some boys in cars were waiting for them. The girls explained that they were going for a ride with the boys, and told us to go on into the movie, then come out when it was over and wait right there for them to pick us up for the walk back to school.

They weren't there when the movie was over. We waited outside the theater for quite awhile, at least it seemed a long time to us. Then we walked down the street, looking in the windows and getting farther from the school all the while. The senior girls and their boy friends finally caught up with us and the scared girls climbed out of the cars, collected us and headed for home as fast as we could go—but it was way past the time that we should've been back and we were all in deep trouble. Out punishment was the *total* cancellation of movie privileges *for the rest of the school year.*

Another lesson in discipline happened soon afterward, after my best friend at the school went for a ride in the ice wagon with the boy who delivered ice to the kitchen. She was caught and expelled from school. I figured she was lucky. I would have been glad to be expelled—only I knew that I wouldn't dare face my dad if I were.

During Christmas vacation I went to some Bingham Canyon basketball games with my gang, and there I saw a tall, handsome blonde boy, Chuck Roberts, who was playing on the town team. He had lived in Bingham Canyon all his life, too, and I'd known him all that time but had never thought he was anybody special. Now, all at once, he seemed to have grown up and gotten terribly good looking. The other kids said he'd been the best player on the football team that fall, too, and I thought he was about the neatest thing I'd ever seen.

I raved about him to my girl friends and tried my best to make him notice me; but he already had a girl friend and I didn't make any headway at all. Anyway I truly had a heavy crush on him and he was in my thoughts and dreams a lot the rest of that school year. Then it was vacation time again and I went home with two firm resolutions in mind: (1) to snare Chuck if I possibly could; (2) *no matter what,* I was never going back to that girls' school.

I had turned sixteen in April and felt completely grown up. I wasn't bad looking and I had good clothes. Too, I was the only kid in Bingham Canyon who had gone away to school during the past two years and that kind of impressed the other kids and made them look up to me. But I still couldn't get Chuck to pay any attention to me. That was a big disappointment to me, but in spite of it I had fun that summer.

A movie company had put in a drive-in theater early that spring, so the big thing was to go to the drive-in. I went quite often, first with one boy and then another. Most of them had old beat-up jalopies to take their dates in and we didn't mind in the least. One boy had an especially junky old Model T; the doors wouldn't open and he had cut the top off, but the engine ran and the wheels turned and we liked it.

One evening, just as he pulled up at the hotel door to take me to the drive-in it began to rain. I ran back into the dining room, pulled a red and white checked oilcloth cover off a table, wrapped it around me and snatched an umbrella from the stand by the door as I went back out. I climbed in over the door, hoisted my big old umbrella over the both of us and we went chugging up the street in the fading daylight. Everybody on the street knew us, and my outfit really set them off. All the way up to the drive-in folks hollered and waved at us, and we hollered and waved back.

What I didn't know was that my dad had seen me go by in my outlandish get-up. Always a dressy man, very particular about how he looked, and polite and well-mannered, he was terribly embarrassed. Afterward, Mom told me how he came storming into the hotel, scolding about the way I was always humiliating him and the family name of Contratto before the whole town. Mom hadn't seen me leave, so she asked him what I'd done now, and when he described my outfit she laughed. That was Mom. She could always see the funny side of things.

I embarrassed my brother Don that summer, too. He had a new girl friend, Dee, from Magna, a little town to the north. I had liked her fine—until the day I saw her wearing my best ring. Mom had given me the ring, a lovely little pearl affair; it was my finest piece of jewelry and I wore it only on the most dress-up occasions.

When Dee and Don came into the parlor one evening and I saw my ring on her engagement finger I spoke right up. "Dee, *where* did you get my ring?" I demanded.

"It isn't yours, it's mine," she said. "Don gave it to me last night."

Poor Don. He would have given anything for a knothole to crawl through just then. And I should have thought a minute —and then kept still until I could talk to him alone. But not me. Oh no! The ring was mine and I wanted it right back. Dee gave it to me, but she was in tears and Don was mad at me and I had upset the whole family by the time I had the little pearl in my possession again.

Don had only "borrowed" the ring, to seal their brand-new engagement of the evening before, meaning all the time to get his sweetheart a ring of her own as soon as he could and give mine back to me. In spite of my bratty interference, he and Dee were later married.

About the end of June I met Lew Ward, also a native of Magna. Lew was nineteen that summer, enough older than I that he had never paid any attention to me before; and anyway he had been in the Navy the past two years, stationed in Guam, and had just been discharged.

We met on a blind date and I found him attractive and interesting. He seemed to like me well enough too, and when he asked me for another date I accepted. My heart and dreams were still with Chuck, who didn't seem to know that I existed, but I wasn't about to pine away waiting for him to wake up to his opportunity to claim my affections.

Anyway Lew was quite a catch for a girl in my sixteen-year-old set. He was an "older man" and had been around and had a car and was a snappy dresser. Besides, I told myself, if Chuck saw me out with Lew he might take notice.

I dated Lew quite a few times that July, but Chuck was still dating the other girl and they ran with a different crowd, so I wasn't getting any place in that direction. Then, in early August, Lew said he thought it would be a good idea if we got married, and I said I guessed it would. And so I was engaged, but I was still hoping for a miracle and that Chuck would ask me for a date. But if he didn't—well, there was that ever present threat of going back to school hanging over me and I had to be prepared.

Dad was as determined as ever to send me back to school, come fall, and I was doing all I could to talk him out of it. Unless I succeeded, there was only *one* way out. Marriage. I didn't want to get married yet; I was too young and having too good a time, but Lew had asked me and I'd said OK, and if I was married I wouldn't have to go back to school.

So that's the way things were until one evening in August when Dad decided to put on one of his Italian dinners. Dad loved to cook Italian foods and he was very good at it, too. So Don asked Dee, and I told Lew he'd just as well come over for it. Come supper time, we took our places at the table. Lew and I sat at the back side of the table, facing the door into the lobby; the boarders had already eaten, so the door was closed for privacy while the family ate.

We were having a fine time over Dad's gourmet meal when someone knocked on the door. Dad, sitting on the front side of the table, answered the knock and I heard someone ask to speak to Ann. Dad stepped back—and I saw Chuck at the door, all dressed up and so good looking. My heart sank, and Chuck's face fell.

"Oh," he said quickly, "I see you have company. Good night, Sir," and he stepped back out of sight.

I wanted with all my heart to run after him and tell him it was all right, that I'd been waiting all summer for him to ask to take me out. But it was too late. He'd seen me sitting there beside Lew, having a good time, and I knew then that I'd lost him forever. (I learned later that some of my girl friends had told him how I was always raving about him, and that I thought he was the greatest, so when he broke up with his steady girl he had come right over to ask me for a date).

Then Lew gave me a nudge and I looked up. His face was black as a thunder cloud. "I think we'd better get married tonight," he hissed at me, and I said I guessed we had. There really didn't seem to be anything else to do. I knew I'd blown it with Chuck, and that I'd have to be heading back to school in less than two weeks if I didn't do *something*. When dinner was over we went out to Lew's car and made some hurried plans.

At first I felt awful. I'd lost out on my chance for a date with Chuck, and I didn't really want to get married, or to leave home for good. I was only sixteen and I wanted more years of dating and playing around with all my good friends; and the little bit of common sense I possessed told me that I should have those years.

Then the daring, impulsive side of me took over and I threw common sense to the winds. I began thinking that, if I did what Lew wanted, I'd be the first kid in my crowd to get married. I always liked to be the big shot of the bunch and this would really be it. The other girls would all look up to me, and they'd envy me the romantic experience of *eloping*, and driving through the night to be married in the morning in some far away place. All at once I was full of romantic feelings and ready for anything.

Lew's plan was for us to drive to Elko, over in Nevada, where the marriage laws were less stringent than Utah's. We'd get married there, and spend our one day and night honeymoon there, and then come home and tell the world, Bingham Canyon anyway, that we had run away and gotten married. I agreed to everything.

But there was one problem. I was wearing Levis, bobby socks and sneakers, my usual garb, but I wanted to be dressed up for my wedding. I didn't dare go back to my room and change, or even try to sneak my good clothes out to the car. Dottie, or someone else, would be almost sure to see me and want to know what was going on. And I knew very well that my parents would put an instant stop to the whole affair if they knew about it.

Lew agreed that I'd better have some different clothes. He said that I looked about twelve or fourteen in my present outfit, and he was afraid we'd have a hard time getting our marriage license. "Let's go over to Lucy's" I said, for I knew that her clothes fit me as well as my own. "She'll loan me everything I need and we can get started. She'll keep still about it, too."

There was no one home at Lucy's, so we went on to Jean's. I didn't change, just slipped the things out to the car, after she had promised, cross her heart, that she wouldn't tell a soul, and away we went.

I was so filled with the whole romantic idea of our elopement, and how the other girls would envy me when they found out about it, that I didn't have any more doubts and fears as we rattled westward toward Elko. And I was really exulting over the way I was getting out of having to go back to school.

What would be only a four or five hour drive to Elko today, took a lot longer in 1948, what with the kinds of roads and cars we had then, and it was morning when we pulled into the town.

We had breakfast and then I went to a filling station restroom to put on my borrowed wedding outfit. The dress was a couple of sizes too big for me, but it did make me look older and more sedate. Then we went to the courthouse, found the place to buy our marriage license, and then on to the judge's office. It was all over in a few minutes—and I was a married woman.

There were still problems, plenty of them. For one, I knew my folks would be worried because I hadn't come home the night before. Right after we left the judge's office I told Lew he'd have to call Mom. At that time in the morning Dad would be at the police station, probably sending out pick-up calls for me, but Mom was sure to be at the hotel and I figured it would be best to tell her first, and let *her* tell Dad.

Lew didn't want to make the call. He thought I should do it, but I finally persuaded him to do it. Mom listened, then made the classic remark for such occasions, "I see. Well I guess you've made your bed, so now you'll have to lie in it." Lew told her we'd be home the next day; and, that over with, we spent the rest of the day looking around, eating snacks and gigling over the fact that we were now Mr. and Mrs. Lew Ward—and nobody knew it but the judge and Mom and us—and probably Dad, but I tried not to think about that.

We put up at a hotel that night, and Lew signed the register "Mr. and Mrs." with a flourish. We drove home the next day and I made sure we didn't arrive at the hotel until mid-afternoon, when Dad was sure to be on duty at the police office. I wasn't afraid to face Mom, but Dad—that was a whole different deal.

Mom told us she was sorry we'd run off, that that wasn't the way she'd planned for me to be married. I was sorry, too, on her account, but not on my own, not yet, and anyway I was in a hurry to get out of town before we ran into Dad. We told Mom that we had to get on over to Magna and tell Lew's mother, and that we'd probably stay there a day or two.

Chapter Eleven

Marriage

There was nothing to be gained by putting off facing Dad any longer; so, much as I dreaded it, after a couple of days in Magna we went back to Bingham Canyon. As I had anticipated, Dad was furious. I guess I had half expected him to spank me, and I was relieved when he didn't; for I hadn't been sure that even being a married woman would spare me that. In spite of everything I still felt that I was his little girl, and I was afraid he felt that way, too.

I was surprised when Mom and Dad finally asked me to go into the parlor, alone, with them. There they told me that they would have the marriage annulled if I would let them. I wouldn't even consider it. I still hadn't had my fling as a runaway bride with the Bingham Canyon kids, and I wasn't about to miss *that*. Besides, to consent to an annullment would be the same as admitting that I'd made a mistake, that I'd been wrong. I wasn't about to do that with my dad. Instead, I'd stay married and show him that I could manage my own life successfully.

After the show-down with my folks was over we set about

telling our friends that we were married. When I went to see Big Helen and told her, she gave me her blessing and some money. My grandmother Lennon looked at me in a queer way, then told me I was only a kid and not dry behind the ears yet, and that she hoped I wouldn't be sorry.

With my Bingham Canyon crowd it was, at first, about like I had expected it to be. For a few days we were celebrities. We walked around town hand in hand, or with our arms around each other—something nice kids didn't dare do in those days unless they were married. The girls looked in envious awe at my plain little wedding band, and everybody was full of questions. The kids teased us and treated us to cokes and sodas and it was all very exciting and satisfying. And then it all fell apart.

By the end of the week posters announcing the change in shows at the Princess were more exciting to our friends than the stale news that Ann and Lew had run off and gotten married. And the next week school started and I watched my friends go off to Copperton. Most of them had two more years to go before graduation—and I should have been with them. That was when it hit me—I'd made an awful mistake.

I admitted it to myself then, that what I'd thought was love for Lew was only being in love with love, and romance, and wanting to show off before my peers. And I knew Lew was beginning to feel the same way. We were both too young to know what was best for us and we both had a great deal of growing up yet to do. I did a lot of mine in that hard hour of facing facts. I had refused to let my parents annul the marriage. Even then, it wasn't too late but I was not about to go to them and chicken out, not to Dad, anyway. *I'd stay married and make it work.*

Fortunately for both of us we had a lot of things to do right away. We had been staying at the Knight Hotel but I knew we would have to make different arrangements—and soon. Dad was kind and generous in many ways, but he wasn't about to support a couple of cocky kids who wouldn't listen to him when he tried to tell them what was good for them.

So we had to look for a place to live; and Lew, who had been living on his Navy severance pay, was about broke and had to get a job. Houses or apartments that we could afford were scarce in Bingham Canyon, but we finally found a tiny house, located at the back of a slightly larger house next to the street. A lovely elderly lady who had recently come from England owned both houses and lived in the front one. I think the back one had originally been a garage, but she, or someone, had remodeled it into a house. The result was a tiny livingroom, bedroom and kitchen, none of them much bigger than a closet. It was furnished, and the rent was low, so we moved in and set up housekeeping.

Lew found a job in one of the mines and we began learning what it was like to live on a miner's salary and make ends meet. Until then I didn't know how good I'd had it, those first sixteen years of my life. What we had to face wouldn't have been *easy* under the best of circumstances—but for me it was *awful*. I didn't know the first thing about cooking or keeping house. At the hotel I'd never had to do it, and Mom, with hired help to take care of all that, hadn't had time to teach me.

But I was confident, of course, that I could do it—and even do a super job of it. Right off I asked Lew's mother for her recipe for making bread. She baked lovely bread and she wrote it all down for me, the ingredients and the quantities. Then she wrote "mix well," and under that, "knead and let set two hours. Make into loaves, let set two hours and bake."

I couldn't find any "knead" in my cupboard and I didn't think I ought to take time, at that stage, to go to the store after some, so I just covered my wad of dough and let it set two hours. It just sat. But I went ahead to the next step and put it in the pans and let it set two more hours. It still didn't do anything. Maybe what it needed was heat to make it puff up into nice big loaves, so I put the heavy little wads in the oven and baked them. Then I threw the rock-hard lumps out and went after more information.

We had been given an electric toaster, so one day I decided to make some French toast. I had no idea how one made it but it was one of my favorite eatables; so I called Dad and asked him how to make it. "Beat up an egg and add milk and a pinch of salt," he told me. "Then soak your bread in the mix—and that's all there is to it."

I followed his directions, then dropped the wet slices of

bread into my toaster. My next call to Dad was to ask him how the clean the toaster. He didn't say anything for a minute—and then he gasped, "I'd just throw it out."

Come my first wash day, I gathered all my soiled clothes and linens and dumped them, whites and colors, into the washing machine: towels, socks, sheets, teatowels, everything, including a new red blouse of mine, went in together. Lew was upset over the decided pink tint of his best white shirts and I wasn't happy with my dingy pink sheets, towels, and other garments.

I had made up my mind that I was going to be an economical housekeeper and a sharp shopper for supplies. After taking out money for rent and other absolute neccessities there wasn't an awful lot left for groceries and household supplies. Since I had plenty of time to go to the store everyday, I bought only enough food for a day at a time. That way my week's grocery money seemed to last longer. Every day I bought just two eggs, one for Lew's breakfast and one for mine. After a while the grocer tried to explain to me that eggs were cheaper by the dozen and that I could actually save some money by buying them that way.

Everybody was kind and helpful, but I had an awful lot to learn.

I don't know what I would have done if it hadn't been for Big Helen and my landlady, Mrs. Fennel. Big Helen seemed to guess how things were, although I was too proud to tell her, and every now and then she gave me something pretty, or useful, or both. And Mrs. Fennel was always doing nice things for me, bringing over something tasty to eat and showing me how to do things. I loved her and did whatever I was able to for her. She had long, lovely hair and I was good with hair, so I'd do hers whenever she wanted me to and we enjoyed each other.

One awfully windy afternoon I was doing her hair in my tiny livingroom. The wind seemed to be getting stronger by the minute and papers and cans and other trash were flying by the window. Pretty soon we heard a queer ripping sound, and then big pieces of boards and tar paper went sailing by. "Oh, oh," I said, "There goes somebody's roof."

When I finished her hair we went out into the yard—and

then saw that the roof was mine. Not the whole roof, but quite a big patch of it. The little shack had leaked some anyway, so it was somewhat better after Mrs. Fennel had the blown-off patch repaired.

Lew and I both tried, those first hard months of our marriage, but facing the realities we were up against was tough. Until then I had always had a nice home, good food, pretty clothes, jewelry, perfume, plenty of spending money—just about anything I wanted. Lew had had only himself to look after and could spend his money on clothes, his car, or however he liked. Now, suddenly, we were counting pennies, stretching Lew's salary as far as two inexperienced kids could, and going without shows and cokes and so many of the things we had always taken for granted.

I was a little too old to take up the ore business again, even though I could still pass for a twelve-year-old in my usual Levis and bobby socks. So I found a job in one of the local bakeries for awhile, and when that didn't work out I helped Mom in the hotel office whenever she needed me. Naturally, I grew apart from the girls my own age. They were busy in school and with school affairs, and I was out of all that. It was a lonely time for me.

Lew and I didn't seem to belong with the other young married folks in town; they were older than we were and had children and more mature interests and we didn't have much in common. We didn't belong to any church either, so we had no opportunities in that direction. Lew could occasionally go down to one of the bars of an evening and find some buddies to help him while away the time, but Bingham Canyon girls, married or single, didn't go to bars in those days.

I spent many a lonely evening, that winter, until Christmas when Lucy dropped out of school and got married. Then we were a foursome again and could spend our evenings together at her place or mine, or save our pennies and go to the show together once in awhile. Toward spring another newly married young couple moved to town and we had a "crowd" again. Things began to get a little better.

Most of my long-time friends graduated from high school the second spring after my marriage, but I didn't go to any of

the graduation affairs. My first child was due in a few weeks—
and anyway I couldn't bear to see Jean and all the other girls in
their lovely new dresses, walking across the auditorium stage
before an admiring audience to receive their diplomas—and
knowing it would never happen to me.

Chapter Twelve

Big Helen

Sue was born early that summer and dear old Dr. Frazier, who had delivered more than 4000 babies during the 40 years he practiced in Bingham Canyon, officiated. A few years earlier (1939–1941) he had taken time out to go with Admiral Byrd, as senior medical officer, on his expedition to the Antarctic. We had truly been fortunate to have so good and kind a man for one of our doctors during all those years, and I'm still proud of the fact that he was my doctor.

After Sue came I was plenty busy with bottles and diapers and all that goes with a baby. I could no longer make a little money outside my home and we were stretching Lew's pay check farther than ever—and then farther still when Shar was born fifteen months later.

I didn't go down town every day any more; I was too busy and it was too much of an effort. Now I went only when I had to. One hot afternoon I was struggling up the street from the grocery store to our house with the two babies and a sack of groceries. It was quite a job, carrying Shar and the grocery sack in one arm and dragging my short-legged toddler Sue along with my other hand.

About an hour later, when Casey showed up at my door with the biggest and best baby buggy the Bingham Merc carried in stock, I knew that blessed Big Helen had seen my plight and, as usual, had come to the rescue. After that I fairly sailed up and down the street with both girls and the groceries, too, all neatly stowed in the elegant carriage.

I still went to see Big Helen as often as she'd let me; and I now understood the reason she kept my visits short and much more infrequent than I liked. And one day she told me how she had gotten into her particular business.

She had grown up in a little town where she had had friends and good times, much the way it had been with me in Bingham Canyon. She and her high school class had come to the end of their Junior year and the prom was coming up. A very special boy had asked her to go to the prom with him and she was in the clouds over that and wanted to look extra pretty for the occasion. So she asked her mother for a new dress for the dance—and was told the one she had was good enough.

"It was an old dress," Big Helen told me, "a hand-me-down from a cousin and an ugly thing." She made up her mind that she wouldn't wear the old dress, and she couldn't bear to tell the special boy she couldn't go to the prom with him—so she ran away to Salt Lake City.

She had no money, she couldn't find a job and, only a fifteen-year-old girl, hungry and homeless, was walking the streets one night when she was accosted by a pimp. He offered her food and a job and she wound up as a call-girl. The years passed and she became well-to-do, the madame of her own house.

I don't remember how she happened to come to Bingham Canyon, but she had been there since before I was born and she had always been interested in me, and then in Dottie when she came along. My mother told me later that Big Helen had told her, while we were yet tiny girls, that she must never let us go without anything we needed, or wanted badly. "If you can't afford to get them nice things just let me know. I'll get them anything, just anything. They must never do what I did," she said.

She always sent her gifts to the hotel by Casey, or by one of the taxicab drivers. She never brought them herself, or went to any of the Bingham Canyon homes, and now I understood that, too.

Looking back on those days now, I wonder if Big Helen didn't keep a watchful eye on just about everything that went on in our town. Anyway I think it likely that my dad owed his life to her on at least one occasion. R. J. Contratto, Chief of Police of Bingham Canyon, was fast, strong and tough, but fair; and the townspeople looked up to him and respected him. Law breakers and would-be lawbreakers feared him, too. He had had a run-in recently with a young Puerto Rican who had come off second best. Vowing revenge, and knowing he was no match for Dad, the young tough gathered *four* of his friends and hid out in the narrow space between Nick's and the 520.

It was just dark when Dad left the hotel and started down the street. As he passed the corner of the 520 the five Puerto Ricans, armed with knives, jumped him. He knocked two of them down and was barely holding his own with the other three when the door opened and Big Helen handed him a broom. That evened things up a bit and, by the time help arrived, he had put all five of his attackers down. He then handcuffed and marched them across the street to the jail.

A year or so after she gave me the baby buggy, Big Helen became quite ill. I went to see her, of course, and found her in bed in her bedroom. I had always visited her in her big kitchen, and so had never been in her bedroom before. The kitchen and her room were side by side at the front of the long, narrow building, each with its own door opening onto the sidewalk. The "girls" rooms opened off a long hallway that ran all the way to the back.

The door between the kitchen and Big Helen's room had always been closed, but that day it was open, and no one closed it after I went in to sit beside my friend's bed and talk with her. A few minutes later a man came into the kitchen to talk to the girls sitting there. Then he looked through the open door and saw me; right away he came barging in and said, "Hi, Helen," then pointing to me he said, "That's the one I want, I'll take her."

The girls and Casey were quick about getting the fellow out

and the door closed. Then, with tears in her eyes, Big Helen said, "Honey, you must *never* come here to see me again." She meant it and I understood, so with tears in my own eyes, I hugged her and kissed her goodbye. That was the last time I saw her, for soon after that Big Helen, the lady with the biggest heart in Bingham Canyon, died in Salt Lake City.

Chapter Thirteen

Many Changes

After Shar was born we had to have more room. Mrs. Fennel's little house just wasn't big enough for four people, so we found a larger apartment farther down the street. It was on the top floor of a three-story building and climbing two flights of stairs with two babies, groceries and supplies wasn't easy but I managed it.

I knew when we moved in that Woody's undertaking parlor was on the first floor, in the front of the house and directly beneath us. I didn't think it would bother me, but it did. I kept thinking about it, those dead people down there in the rooms below, and it really upset me, especially at night. Every time I left the building, or came in, I had to go right past Woody's work room to reach the stairs and it got more unbearable all the time. After three months of living above the undertaking establishment I found another apartment and we moved again.

Shar was five when Danny was born. A few months later we moved to Kearns, a little town about 25 miles northeast of Bingham Canyon. There we had a brand new little house and I enjoyed that—but all the time things were getting worse and worse between Lew and me. We had both known for a long time that we had made a big mistake in getting married so young, and both of us had tried hard to make a go of it.

I had tried especially hard because I had been so headstrong about the marriage in the first place. When my folks had begged me to have it annulled I had refused, so now I couldn't let it fail and prove me wrong. By then, even though my parents had separated and Dad had gone to Guam, I still wanted to show them that we had known what we were doing and that they had been mistaken in thinking we didn't. Besides, the girls loved their father. They loved both of us and wanted us together and I didn't want to hurt them.

Eventually, however, the constant arguments and disagreements became unbearable and my health began to fail. "Nerves" were getting the best of me, so, after fourteen years I decided to call it quits. That decision, the separation, and finally the divorce, were very unhappy experiences.

I kept the children and set out to make a living and a new life for us. The relief from the daily quarreling helped, my health improved and, in time, life looked bright again. By Hallowe'en we were settled into our life without Lew. I had found a night job in a bakery in Kearns, two miles from where we were living, and we were managing quite well.

Holidays were always fun for me and I especially enjoyed Hollowe'en, with its opportunity to dress up in wild, colorful costumes and parade around. That year I dressed as a witch— and really *looked* like one by the time I was all made up. I hopped in my car and set out to drive to work. Half way there my car quit. It was almost full dark by then and I began flashing my lights for help.

In those days passing motorists would always stop to give aid to people in a stalled car and, shortly, an oncoming car stopped and a man got out and walked toward my car in the glare of his headlights. I climbed out of my car and went around to the engine to explain the way it had sputtered and died. By then I had forgotten my Hallowe'en get-up, and when the poor fellow got a good look at me he actually turned white.

One occasion during that part of my life I will never forget.

It was my birthday and my little girls, only about eight and ten, decided to have a surprise birthday party for me. They asked some of the neighbors to come and bring a birthday cake, and Grandma Lennon to bring the ice cream.

I paid them a weekly allowance for washing dishes and helping keep the house clean and they had saved their money for a long time so they could buy me a pretty dress. In those days one could buy really nice voile dresses, all ruffled and flowery and feminine, for $2.98 or $3.98. I loved that dress and wore it until it practically fell off me.

Even little Danny had a gift for me, an identification bracelet with a tiny picture of the three of them attached. I suspect that Grandma Lennon had a big hand in that. I still have it and it is one of my choicest treasures, along with the sweet memory of that million-dollar party.

After a time we moved to Salt Lake City, where I went to work in a Woolworth store coffee shop. Of course I had my moments there, too. One very busy lunch hour I got a bit addled, trying to handle too many orders at once, and served a man a *soda straw* with a bowl of chili soup. He was very nice about it, just called me back and said, "Honey, I don't mind sucking broth through a straw, but how do you get a *bean* through one?" In my dismay and confusion I had to stop and think a minute as to whether I should give him a malt straw or a spoon.

In spite of my poor beginning I soon worked up to manager of the fountain and lunch counter. I liked the work and enjoyed being the "boss." Shortly after that the store changed managers. The new head's name was Norman Herrick and he came from Wyoming. I liked his looks, in fact I thought him very handsome as he was tall and dark and dressed well, but from the start we didn't get along as co-workers in the store. We disagreed and argued a lot, and one day I told him that the other "dime store" in town paid better wages and had more help at its fountain.

"Why don't you get a job at the other store, then?" he asked.

"I'll just do that," I said, and quit Woolworth's on the spot.

Well, I didn't get a job at the other store, but I did get one right away at a factory in the city. So I was safely employed when Norman called me a few days later and asked me to come back to Woolworth's. We met and talked it over, calmly for once, and *agreed* that it was best for us to work in separate establishments—and *then* he asked me for a date. I was thrilled and said yes.

On our first date we took my kids along and went to a drive-in movie, where we had such a good time that we arranged for another date before we said goodnight. We soon fell into a sort of pattern. During the week Norman ate supper at our place nearly every evening. He furnished the groceries and I prepared them, and we laughed a lot and had good times.

On Saturday nights we went out alone, to a good restaurant for dinner and then to a show or some other kind of entertainment. Norm was always very nice to the waitresses—too nice, I thought. It was only his way, for he was always nice to everyone, but I was falling in love with him and that made me possessive and jealous. Evidently I displayed my feelings so much that he decided I needed to be shown how silly I was acting. That night when the waitress came to our table he told her he was sorry but he couldn't place our order because I wouldn't let him talk to waitresses.

That made me furious. I told him I'd never speak to him again and that I was leaving, right now. He immediately slid off his chair onto his knees in front of me, and the waitress and all the diners in the restaurant, and begged my forgiveness. Everyone was laughing and enjoying the odd little comedy and I was in a bad spot. I told him I forgave him, and I even kept calm and collected while he ordered our dinner and we ate it. But after we left the restaurant he found himself in trouble.

Awhile later it was Norman's turn to be embarrassed. I used to love to try to improve on nature and was always experimenting with the newest fads. I was only twelve when I talked Mom into letting me "henna" my hair. After that my friends never knew what I'd be the next day, or the next week, a blonde, a redhead or a gal with midnight tresses.

Naturally, when fake eyelashes came along I had to have a pair. A friend, Nadine, and her husband, John, used to make a foursome with Norm and me. We were going together to

96

dinner one evening, and that afternoon Nadine and I each bought a pair of long, curling eyelashes. We glued them on at my house and they looked so romantic that we decided we'd have to wear them to dinner with Norm and John.

All went well and we were very satisfied with ourselves until the waitress set my bowl of soup down in front of me and one of my gorgeous eyelashes fell in the soup and floated there for all to see. Norm looked at me as if he were seeing little wiggly things and Nadine and I fled to the ladies lounge, where I took off my other eyelash and she took off both of hers.

Another time I tried fake fingernails. They were guaranteed not to fall off, once you had them glued on, so I wore a gay red set to church with Norm and was sitting sedately in my seat when one of them popped off, flew over the seat in front of me and landed in the powder-blue lap of the plump lady sitting there. She was so startled at sight of that blood-red finger nail that she jumped to her feet and looked wildly around. I quickly put my hands together in my lap, under my scarf, and tried to look as if I hadn't noticed anything unusual.

Except for such episodes, which we soon laughed about, we got along remarkably well, Norm and I, and had a lot of fun and good times together. Norm had been married before, too, and was divorced and had two young sons, Steve and Jay, who lived with their mother. He liked my children and they liked him and all went smoothly for several months.

On Christmas Eve Grandma Lennon had a family dinner and invited Norm and me. Norm picked me up at my home and we headed for Grandma's house, but on the way he drove into a parking lot beside a bowling alley and asked me to marry him. I said I would and he put a lovely diamond on my engagement finger. Then we dashed on to Grandma's and told her and Grandpa. They were pleased and we were so happy. *This*, I thought to myself, is what promising to marry a man and becoming engaged *should* be like, and I was very grateful that it had finally happened to me.

But the best thing Norm did for me during that period was to take me to church with him. At that time I was totally confused about religion. In Bingham Canyon Mom, a Mormon, had sent Dottie and me to her church, although I had usually ended up at the home of one of my friends instead. Dad, a Roman Catholic, had sent me to the Catholic girls school that I had disliked so much. There I had had to go to services, where I had done what my schoolmates did, mostly kneeling and standing, kneeling and standing, with none of it meaning anything significant to me.

In Norm's church I began to learn about the real meaning of religion for the first time and a whole new world opened up for me. I realized then that I had needed this knowledge and assurance for a long time, so I answered the altar call invitation and went forward and was saved.

That experience made a different person of me, and in the way I looked at things. It made me more compassionate, more tolerant of other people's faults and mistakes. Perhaps, if I had been a Christian before I married Lew, I could have been a more understanding wife, less given to temper and impatience, and things might have worked out for us. It was too late to do anything about that now as it was all in the past, but I had the rest of my life ahead of me and I meant, with God's help, to live it very differently.

With my usual impulsiveness I had embraced salvation, and the Christian way of life, with all confidence that I could immediately begin to live a new life, a Christian life, according to all the rules of loving my neighbor as myself. The truth was that I had a lot to learn, and it wasn't going to be either quick or easy.

A few months after the Christmas of our engagement Norm was transferred to a Woolworth store in Montana. As rapidly as he could he made arrangements for a home for us, but it was the next year, 1963, before he had everything ready and could come for us. We left Salt Lake in his car and stopped in an Idaho town long enough to go to the courthouse, buy a license and be married by a lady judge.

The little Montana town was so different from our former home, and by the next summer my girls were so homesick for Salt Lake that they decided to go back there and live with their father, who had also remarried. Danny stayed with us, and Norm's boys spent their summers with us until they were grown.

Chapter Fourteen

My salvation experience had shown me that I was a sinner and that there was much in my life that needed to be changed. It wasn't easy; I had lived too many years for myself, loved having my own way and doing as I pleased. Now I saw that all that was wrong and I wanted to change, to be the person that the Lord wanted me to be. Norman was a big help to me, but I still had a long and difficult struggle ahead.

The move to Montana was a big change for me in many ways. It was not only a different kind of country and a different climate, but I had to make new friends and we had to find a church that preached the Bible and met our needs. All this took time and the disruption was not good for me, a very new Christian. Then, just as things were smoothing out for me and I was feeling comfortably settled, the girls decided to go back to their father in Salt Lake and I lost my Grandpa Lennon.

My father, then living in Salt Lake, called to tell me that Grandpa had died and that Grandma wanted me to come to the funeral. When I told Norman and he checked the bus schedules and told me that the only way I could get to Salt Lake in time was by plane I panicked. No way was I *ever* going to get on an airplane, even though I knew that I *had* to be with Grandma in her time of loss. Norman went ahead and bought my plane ticket, helped me pack and drove me to the airport.

I was crying as I started up the ramp to board the plane. Halfway up I turned to look back at Norman and Danny. They waved and smiled and I almost ran back to them, but I knew if I did Norm would just take me right back to that ramp. Then the stewardess saw my fear and took my hand and promised me that everything would be all right. She got me into the plane, strapped me into my seat and told me she would sit beside me as soon as we were ready to go.

I was barely able to talk by the time she was strapped into the seat beside me, but I managed to explain to her that, if she would see to it that none of the passengers left their seats to go to the bathroom or anything, maybe we'd make it all right. I had the awful feeling that, unless everybody stayed in their seats and kept quiet, the whole thing would fall out of the sky. She insisted that I shouldn't worry, that the plane had made the trip many, many times and such a thing hadn't happened yet.

But I worried anyway. When we landed and I was about to dash off the plane and get my feet on solid ground again, the stewardess took my hand and said, "Now, that wasn't so bad, was it?" "It was horrible," I assured her, "and I'm taking the bus home."

Grandma was so glad to see me. I was even glad that I'd stayed on that plane long enough to go to her, for we had always been very close, and she knew how much I had loved Grandpa. After the funeral she kept thinking of reasons why I should stay another day, and then another, but I finally had to tell her goodbye and board my bus for home. When she died, a few years later, after we had moved to California, Norman drove me to Salt Lake for her funeral, and I was comforted to know that she was buried beside Grandpa, in a beautiful Salt Lake City cemetery.

Not long after Grandpa's funeral Norman was quite suddenly transferred to the Assistant managership of a big Woolworth store in San Diego. We had never lived in a really large city before and we found it frightening: the traffic, the hordes of people, the sheer size of the store where Norm would be working. When we first saw the store, acres and acres, so it seemed, of aisles and counters, we both felt lost and lonely. "Oh Honey," I whispered to him, "I wish we had enough money to go home to Salt Lake." He replied with a heartfelt "Me too."

Of course we had to stay, and it really didn't take us long to feel right at home. We found a nice house on the beach overlooking the Pacific before Norm's boys came to spend the summer with us. We went into the ocean every day and soon became quite expert, or so we thought, at jumping waves and swimming in the surf. Almost every evening we had picnics on the beach and congratulated ourselves on being so lucky as to live in California.

All too soon Norm was transferred again, this time to Hollywood. We regretted leaving our comfortable beach home and the ocean, especially when we found that housing in Hollywood was so expensive that all we could afford was an apartment.

It seemed to take longer to make friends there. Maybe it was because no one seemed to stay in one place long enough to get acquainted. So it helped a lot when, soon after we were settled, Norm's parents came out from North Platte, Nebraska, to visit us and took an apartment right above us. They stayed two months, helping us over the worst part of that move.

Of course we wanted to show them a good time and I volunteered to take them sightseeing, to China Town and all the other nearby interesting places they'd heard about. Since I had been to China Town and the other places with Norm at the wheel, I felt confident that I could handle the driving and the traffic as long as I stayed out of *downtown* Los Angeles, that is. That downtown area scared me almost out of my wits.

After Norm had left for work one morning I loaded Dad and Mom Herrick into the car and we headed out. All went well for awhile and we enjoyed our drive until, somewhere, I took a wrong turn. Very shortly I knew we were in trouble. So did Norm's father. He sat up very straight, took a good look at the suddenly very heavy traffic, said, "Oh oh, we're almost in downtown Los Angeles," and began chewing hard on his cigar.

Being lost in the heart of Los Angeles was even more scary than running through the dim old Bingham Canyon tunnel, or watching a Frankenstein movie at the old Princess, or any of the other frightening things that had ever happened to me. Thousands of cars and trucks were rushing along on either side of me, ahead of me and behind me, and all that I could do was rush along with them and pray that we didn't get clipped or bumped or smashed, and that I didn't clip or bump or smash somebody else. I just sort of froze to the wheel and sat there in my little niche in that speeding sea of vehicles.

We had put a good many miles behind us before I found a stretch of highway where the traffic was light enough that I could turn off and head into a service station. We got ourselves straightened out there, and finally on the way to China Town again, by way of less congested streets. By the time we arrived it was well past noon and Norm's father was chewing up his third cigar.

Norm had been manager of the other Woolworth stores where he had worked and, after he got used to the size of the big California establishments, he wanted to be manager again. Convinced that there was no immediate prospect of being promoted where he was, he began to look elsewhere. When he found an opening in a big Safeway Drugstore in Los Angeles he took it, only to be transferred shortly to another Safeway Drug in Placentia, a bustling suburb of Los Angeles. Each move had been a step up for him, with a better salary, and this time we were able to afford a pretty home with a lovely yard and a swimming pool.

What with all the moving and getting used to new communities, new stores and new people, we hadn't gone regularly to church in a long time. In fact we hardly ever went at all, and my Christian growth had suffered badly through all the changes. Now it looked as if we might stay quite awhile in our new location and we began visiting churches again, looking for one where the word of God was taught and we could feel at home.

After awhile we found a Baptist church that seemed solidly based on the Bible and its people very friendly. One couple in particular, Don and Betty Winters, were so warmly welcoming that we were impressed. They invited us to their home, took us sightseeing and helped us in many ways.

Betty was soon my best friend. We saw each other almost every day, at my home or hers, and usually did our shopping together. Betty, who knew the city well, nearly always took her car and did the driving. Then one day, to sort of equalize things, I insisted on taking my car. We went to a big mall and I parked and we spent the afternoon in the stores. When we finally headed back to the parking lot we had, as usual, forgotten where we had left the car. Even worse, we had forgotten that we came in my car. Loaded with packages and bundles, we searched that whole big parking lot from end to end, up and down every row of parked cars—and couldn't find Betty's car anywhere.

Worn out and panicky, Betty finally turned to me and said she was going to call the police and report her car stolen. When she opened her purse to get a dime she saw that her keys weren't there. That convinced her. "Oh, Betty," she gasped, "I must've left the keys in the car, so it was easy for someone to take it." Cars stolen from parking lots was an everyday occurrence there.

But when she fished for a dime to call the police, and found she didn't have one, I opened my bag to get one—and saw *my* car keys. "Betty," I shrieked, "We came in my car today, remember?" And I waved the keys in her face. Then we both sat right down on the pavement and laughed till we cried.

It was Betty who made the big difference in my Christian life. Faithful to God, His church and its works, she was the most caring, compassionate person I have ever known. She set a splendid example in Christian living for me, and helped me over many a hard place in the months and years to come. Danny, Norm and I began going regularly to church and helping in the various phases of its work. We enjoyed it, felt much better about ourselves and made many good friends.

Norm's boys still spent their summers with us and his parents visited us as often as they felt up to making the long trip. Those were happy years, but times were changing and they brought changes into our lives, too.

Norm's former wife had married again and moved to Nebraska, to Farnam, a little town about forty miles from North Platte. The fall the boys were to start to high school Norm realized how much he was missing by not being near enough to go to their football games and other important school activities. Danny, too, was ready for high school and we thought it would be best for him if we were permanently settled somewhere, so he could graduate from the same school in which he enrolled as a freshman. In Norm's present work we never knew where we would be from one year to the next.

Then too, Dad and Mom Herrick were getting old and we knew that soon they would no longer be able to travel so far to visit us. So Norm began talking about moving back to Nebraska. After all, he had grown up on a farm south of North Platte, and he had two brothers still in that part of the country, one in North Platte and the other near Farnam.

I didn't want to leave California, and Betty, and our church. We had developed a pattern, a way of life that I loved, but Norman was the family provider and I wanted what he wanted, what seemed best for him. Before long we were on our way to North Platte.

We had saved some money and wanted to invest it in something we could do together, a business of our own. I liked restaurant work and had had enough experience at the Woolworth fountain and lunch counter to enable me to run one of my own, and Norm was a good businessman and manager. We bought the Elletts Tastee Treat, remodeled it into "Betty's Tastee Treat," and opened for business.

Chapter Fifteen

Horse Tradin'

It was at this period in our lives that I learned I had married a horse trader. I had seen evidence of this side of Norman from time to time, but nothing really serious until we were settled in North Platte. Born and raised on a farm but long ago transplanted to the city and business management, he had done very well. But now, back again in the farming country of Nebraska, his farmer and "trader" tendencies surfaced.

We had hired a very efficient and dependable woman named Janice to help us run the restaurant. She was so good that, with her help, I was soon almost running the Tastee Treat by myself and Norman didn't have to spend all of his time at the business. Although he helped out at rush times, he still had a good deal of free time to be away from the place, time to give rein to his horse tradin' instincts.

He began spending time at the big Western Livestock Sales Barn where, every Tuesday, thousands of head of cattle, pigs and horses were sold at auction. He loved being with the farmers, ranchers and feeders who came to buy and sell. And one day he couldn't resist buying.

The first I knew of *that* was when he came back to the restaurant with the back of his pickup full of newly weaned baby pigs. They'd been a real bargain, he said, and there was money in pigs, so he'd bought them. All he had to do now was to find a place to keep and care for them until he could turn them at a profit. It was early spring and very chilly of nights, so he thought it would be a good idea to fix a little pen in the back of the Tastee Treat for them.

At that time we were living in a large room behind the restaurant kitchen; but Norm didn't mean a pen *at* the back of the building—he meant a pen *in* the back of the building, in our living quarters.

I blew up. I was not only horrified at the idea of keeping pigs in the restaurant, but I was certain he had wasted, thrown away, the money he had paid for the little porkers. I told him that there was NO WAY that we'd keep the pigs there. Someone would find out about it, I said. How could they help it, the way the hungry little things were squealing? And we'd not only be kicked out of the restaurant business but blacklisted from ever running another eatery of any kind, anywhere.

Very disappointed in me, Norm took his bargains back to the sales barn to find feed and shelter for them—and within the hour sold them to someone for $200 more than he paid for them.

Soon after that Norm decided to go into the pig business with his brother Wilbur, who farmed near Farnum. They kept the pigs in a good-sized pen enclosed by an electric fence. The restaurant was closed one day a week, to give us time to catch our breath, and on one of those days Norm asked me to go along with him to deliver a large metal pig feeder to the farm.

At the pig lot he backed the pickup up close to the fenceline to make it easier to unload the feeder into the lot. Then they decided not to walk the rather long distance to turn off the battery, the source of power for the fence. Instead, they said, they'd just let the fence wire down on the ground and be careful not to touch it as they hefted the feeder across it.

That feeder looked pretty big and unwieldy as they began to slide it out of the pickup and I thought I'd better lend a hand. As I hopped out of the cab and came to help they warned me not to step on the fence wire. "You'll get an awful jolt if you do," they said, and I promised to be careful.

The three of us pulled and hauled at the feeder until we had it lifted clear of the pickup. Then helpful Betty, shifting her feet to get a better balance for the last big lift, stepped on the hot wire. Since all three of us had hold of the metal feeder, the contact not only threw a whammy of a jolt into me but into both of the men at the same time. We instantly lost our grips on the feeder, which seemed to leap into the air, then flip upside down and land on its top below us. Our numbed arms hanging at our sides, we stood and watched it roll on down the hillside.

As summer came on the weather turned very hot. We didn't mind it in our air-conditioned cafe, but it was far too hot for the deal Norm arranged for Janice and me in the little eating room attached to the Western Sales Barn. Hundreds of men: truckers, buyers, sellers and visitors, patronized the small hamburger shop in the big sales pavilion.

Norm, who had become friendly with the owner of the sale barn, had met him down town on Monday and found him quite upset because the people who operated the little cafe had suddenly quit and there was no one to handle the fast food business at the sale the next day. "Oh, don't worry," my good husband told him. "My wife will take care of it for you."

He came back to the Tastee Treat and told Janice and me about it. If we'd take it over for tomorrow, he said, we could probably have the business on a regular one-day-a-week basis, and he thought it would pay us well to take it on. I agreed, and we packed up our supplies, made eight gallons of iced tea and drove to the sale barn the next morning.

In a short time we were set up for business—but that was the day the thermometer hit 110 in the shade—and there was no air conditioning in that hot, airless little cafe. The hotter it got the thirstier our customers became. As Janice and I rushed back and forth, trying to keep up with the iced tea demand, we were wiping sweat from our faces and our streaming eyeglasses and I told Janice that, if only someone had invented windshield wipers for glasses, we might have been able to work a little faster.

We still had some hamburgers and pie left when, along in

the afternoon, we ran out of iced tea. The sale still had several hours to run and I suppose we could have sent out for more ice and instant tea. But we didn't, for all our usual cheery zip and goodwill had drained away with the gallons of perspiration we'd shed that blazing afternoon. So we just packed up all our supplies and equipment and headed back for the blessed coolness of the Tastee Treat.

Norm took a look at our loaded pickup and said, "Honey, you didn't need to bring all that stuff back here. No would would have taken it if you'd left it there until next week."

"I know that," I said, "but there isn't going to be any 'next week.' We've quit."

Still true to his horse tradin' bent, Norm one day came driving an ugly old tractor home. That was after we'd bought a nice house in a good part of town. That old tractor looked to me like it had been put together by a crazy man out of barnyard junk and I was ashamed of it, sitting out there on our nice back lawn. But Norm was proud of it. It was a good old machine, he said, and all it needed was a little fixing up and painting, and then he could sell it for a good profit.

By then I should have learned that all Norm's deals seemed to turn out well. But each one of them frightened me and I was certain every time that he'd lose all the money he'd paid out, and I knew we couldn't afford that. When I fussed and scolded he'd just say, "Trust me, Betty," and then go ahead and make a profit on his latest "hoss trade."

He sold the old tractor at a nice profit, but when he acquired a beat-up old jeep a little later he didn't bring it home. I don't remember where he parked it while he worked at fixing it up, probably his father's place, but he got away with it for quite awhile. The whole family knew about it but, at his request, carefully kept it from me—until one day his mother let it slip. She was awfully upset at being the one to give the secret away, and I was upset with Norm over his latest crazy deal—until he resold the refurbished jeep at a good profit.

Finally Norm really got a horse, a beautiful riding horse, but he was afraid to tell me until he had laid some careful plans. First he took me to a nice place for a delicious dinner, and was extra nice to me all the while. Then he drove out to his father's little acreage on the edge of town and said, "See, Betty, we now own a real Arabian horse." I looked at the splendid reddish brown animal—but I didn't share his pleasure and enthusiasm. For one thing, I was afraid of horses; for another, none of us could ride one. As far as I could see the last thing in the world we needed was a horse, even a real Arabian.

This time I *knew* Norm had made a bad deal, and that he'd surely lose everything he'd already put into the animal, and its future upkeep besides. I told him so, but he only said, "Trust me, Betty." He pastured the horse at his father's and went every day to feed and pet his new property. The pasture didn't cost him anything but he had to buy oats and salt for the creature and I objected to that. It would probably eat us out of house and home, I complained, and it wasn't doing us a speck of good.

After a few months Norm sold the horse for quite a lot more than it had cost him—so I was wrong again.

Chapter Sixteen

Problems

All this time our business had been growing and prospering. Danny liked his new school and was doing well; Norm's boys were making good grades and playing on their football team. Everything should have been fine with us. The reason that things weren't as good as they seemed went deep.

Once again we had had to make new friends—and find a new church as soon as we could get around to it, and I'm afraid it was quite awhile before we got around to it. We meant to, but the restaurant kept us too busy—too busy and too tired. Too tired to worship, or pray, or read the Bible or go to church.

Betty, bless her heart, was concerned. She kept writing from California, and calling, urging us to get involved in a good Bible believing church and get back on the right track and not to put it off any longer. And we kept promising to see to it soon. Finally we did take time to visit two or three churches. We liked one of them, a little fundamental Baptist church where the people were friendly and helpful, but we were too busy to go very often.

I realize now that most of our problems lay with me. I was the kind of person who found it hard to delegate duties and authority to others, no matter how capable I knew them to be. I was sure that no one could do things quite as well as I could and, even though I had my fine helper, Janice, I was still trying to do too much at the restaurant, work others could well have done if I had let them.

The biggest problem, though, was that I was leaving the Lord out of my life almost completely and, after my salvation experience, I had a deep down guilt complex about it. I was still living for myself and not for God.

A beautiful poem I ran across later exactly described the way I was living during that hectic, troubled time. I wish I knew who had written it. I would like to thank him, or her.

Take Time to Pray

I got up quite early one morning
And rushed right into the day;
I had so much to accomplish
I took no time to pray.

The problems just tumbled about me,
And heavier came every task;
"Why doesn't God help me?" I wondered.
He said, "Why, you didn't ask!"

I saw naught of joy nor of beauty—
The day sped on grey and bleak;
I asked, "Why won't the Lord show me?"
He said, "Why, you didn't seek!"

I tried to come into God's presence;
I used all my keys at the lock,
God gently, lovingly chided,
"My child, why didn't you knock?"

I woke up quite early this morning
And paused ere entering the day;
There was so much to accomplish
I HAD TO TAKE TIME TO PRAY!

Added to my mental conflict was a physical condition that troubled me. It should have been the easiest and quickest to solve but, true to my usual mixed up way of doing things, I made it much harder than it needed to be. I had been having periodic abdomenal pain for nearly a year and was afraid I had cancer. Everywhere I turned I read something about cancer, or saw something about it on television, so I simply jumped to the conclusion that that was what it had to be. Living with that sickening fear didn't help my other difficulties either.

Norm's mother was the first to notice that I was frequently in pain. "Betty," she said one day, "You'd better see a doctor." I tried to convince her that there was nothing wrong. In my own mind I was positive that it was only a matter of time before I died of cancer anyway, and I felt that I couldn't bear to hear a doctor confirm my own diagnosis.

But Mom Herrick was firm. When she threatened me with, "Betty, if you don't go to a doctor right away I'm going to call your father," I listened. Dad and his second wife, Clara, were living in Salt Lake City then, and I was still as much afraid of him as ever, so I knew I'd better see a doctor.

I hadn't been to a doctor since moving to North Platte, so I asked my sister-in-law, Shirley Herrick, to recommend one, and I shall always be grateful to her for directing me to her own physician, Dr. Robert Ziegler.

Besides having a fine doctor, Shirley also had a lovely fourteen-year-old daughter, Cindy. Cindy and I had taken to each other from the first and she was often at our house, visiting and helping out any way she could. Cindy was a Christian, and very serious about it. She was faithful in attendance at her church and Sunday School and very much concerned when she saw those she loved doing things they shouldn't.

It was my smoking that bothered Cindy the most. It bothered me, too, and had ever since I had joined Norm's church in Salt Lake. I had long been ashamed of the habit and had tried several times to quit. Betty didn't smoke and disapproved of it and I had been careful not to light up a cigarette in her presence, and I couldn't help feeling guilty whenever I was with her and felt myself craving a smoke. Now Cindy was begging me to quit and I was trying, but making very little headway. "Well, we'll just pray about it, Aunt Betty," she said.

"I'll pray every day that you'll be able to quit, and I know you will."

I called Dr. Ziegler and made an appointment to see him the next day. That night I had the worst attack of twisting pain that I'd ever had. Positive that I hadn't long to live, now, I went to the doctor's office to hear the hopeless verdict. Dr. Ziegler was kind and sympathetic. I liked him at once. At least, I thought, it won't be so bad to have *him* tell me that I'm dying of cancer. Instead, after a brief examination, he told me I had a bad case of gall stones and ordered me into the hospital immediately for x-rays and surgery.

Cindy came to see me the day before my surgery. Before she left that evening she said, "I have a prayer list, Aunt Betty, and you're on it. I'm praying for you to get well fast, and that you won't ever smoke again when you come out of the hospital." The child went home then and I smoked another cigarette before I went to sleep. It was my last.

I stood the surgery fine—and never again even wanted a cigarette. Cindy's prayers had worked a miracle.

We had decided to sell the Tastee Treat and Norm had disposed of it at a good price, and then gone to work for the Union Pacific Railroad, which maintains a division point at North Platte where the largest railway hump yard in the world is located. So now, with no daily stint at the restaurant to hold me back, all I had to do was get well.

We now had time to go to church and the future looked bright; but there was still much about God's word and His service that I only dimly understood, a great deal that He still had to teach me. But God knows what it takes to teach some of his stubborn children His will—and my next lesson wasn't long in coming.

I had made a good recovery from my surgery and Norm and I were getting more and more involved in the church and its work, but I still had some problems. For one thing I was entering the change of life period and many things upset me, things I had used to take in stride. For another I still had a nagging conviction that I hadn't yet turned myself fully over to God's will. As a result my nerves took over—and manifested themselves in a strange and frightening way.

One day I found that I could not swallow solid food. Even

liquids were difficult. My throat just closed up tight and wouldn't let anything down. Norm was alarmed and wanted me to see my doctor, but I insisted that it would pass and I'd be all right in a few days. When there was no change he became so insistent that I finally called Dr. Ziegler again.

My good doctor put me back in the hospital for observation and tests, and spent a lot of time with me, explaining my condition and seeing to it that I had the bed rest that I so badly needed. His wife, Bernice, a dietician at the hospital, also came to see me and talk over my problems. She had all my food pureed so I could drink my meals, and helped me in many other ways.

Both the doctor and his wife were understanding, sympathetic and supportive, giving me the encouragement that I needed. Those two fine people were indeed milestones along my road to a full recovery. But, looking back on it now, I can see that the best thing of all was that my illness gave me time to think, to sort out my life and realize what was really wrong— that I was leaving God out and that, after my conversion commitment to Him I had no right to do that. I see now that God sometimes has to strike us down with an injury or illness and *put us on the shelf* for awhile so that we *have* to take time to learn our priorities.

We were temporarily without a pastor at Riverside Church at that time but our new church friends soon found out about my illness and began coming to see me; Lila Shimmin, her daughter Paula Dishman, the two Stoner families and others. The prayers and visits of those good folks were most helpful to me during those days of hospitalization. Through it all of course, my good husband was at my side and Betty and Don Winters were writing and calling from California. I had never felt so surrounded by love and I thanked God for it as I grew closer to Him in my thoughts and knowledge.

After eight days Dr. Ziegler let me go home, on my promise to be very quiet for awhile longer. The Riverside friends still came to see and do for me; Lila, especially was a great help. She was always cheerful and her staunch counseling to "keep on keeping on" encouraged me from day to day. Bernice Ziegler, too kept on coming, directing my diet and overseeing my mental and emotional recovery. She and the doctor are still my good friends, very special people, both of them.

Soon after I was on my feet again Betty began writing to urge Norm and me to go to a Bill Gothard Seminar in Denver. There was nothing like it, she declared, for helping a Christian to live for God, and since it would be held so near to us, only 300 miles away, we couldn't afford to miss it. "It will do more for you than anything else you'll ever have an opportunity to do," she wrote. She was so concerned that she and Don drove back to Nebraska in July to personally persuade us to go.

I'm sure that Betty knew, better than I, that even with my new awareness of my deep down need, I still hadn't let go *all* holds and committed my whole self to God. She and Don had attended a Gothard Seminar in California and, together, they made the experience sound very inviting. Norm was soon enthusiastic about us attending but I was skeptical. It would cost a lot, not only for the Seminar fee but for meals and lodging, and I couldn't see how listening to a series of sermons every day for a week could make all that much difference. We had a regular pastor at Riverside now and Norm and I were attending all services, Sunday morning and evening and mid-week prayer meeting, and I never missed a women's missionary service. I thought we were doing enough.

For Betty's sake I tried to sound enthusiastic, too, but all the while I was thinking that we couldn't actually go, for the Seminar was scheduled for October and Norm's vacation was set up for a different month—and on our railroad you took your vacation when you were told to. I was surprised that Norm hadn't thought of that, but I kept still about it.

Betty and Don went back to California and the summer merged into fall. Then one day Norm phoned me from work. All excited, he said his vacation had been rescheduled for October and covered the very days of the Seminar. "Get ready," he said. "We're going."

Still unconvinced that we were doing the sensible thing, I began to make preparations for the week in Denver. The day before we were to leave home I began to come down with a cold. By the time we checked into our motel the next evening I was miserably sick. My head ached, my body ached, I was feverish and my throat was awfully sore—all the symptoms of the genuine old flu. "Norm, if God really wants me to go and get anything out of that Seminar, He will have to make me well by tomorrow evening," I said.

So we prayed about it right then, and told God exactly that, and then I crawled miserably into bed. I was much better the next morning, and by evening and the opening lecture I had hardly a sniffle left. I had never gotten over a bad cold so quickly before.

The seminar was held in a large auditorium and a huge crowd was in attendance. After that first evening there was no question about it, they couldn't have kept us away. We were in our seats every evening Monday through Friday, all day on Thursday and until noon on Saturday. After day one we wouldn't have missed a session. For the Seminar was all that Betty had promised it would be. It changed our lives, made us see that, if we would live *daily* for Christ, He would take care of everything for us.

"Go home," we were told, "and get involved in a Christ honoring, Christ centered church. Be faithful and follow the Bible's precepts. Put God first in your lives and realize that everything you have belongs to Him. It's not easy to do—but *that* is all there is to it."

Since then I have truly been able to share everything with others, to live for others and not for self. I have been able to overcome all my resentments and jealousies, to forgive everyone who had ever hurt me and *love* them wholeheartedly. Learning to live a consecrated Christian life, and *doing* it, is the greatest thing in the world. I know it now.

We had already found our church, Riverside, and now we truly committed ourselves to doing the Lord's work through His church and through giving of ourselves in everything, our time, our money and our love. Norm entered into the church's visitation program and frequently went calling, seeking people who needed to hear about the Lord and visiting in their homes.

Through visitation he met the Bill Sale family. Sandy, the mother, was already a Christian, Bill and the two boys were not. At Norm's invitation they came to Riverside, liked it and kept coming. Before long Bill and the boys answered the altar call and were saved. They have since been among our most faithful members, and Sandy has been church organist for quite awhile. It has been a blessing to watch the growth of this family, spiritually, and to know that we, Norm and I and many others among our number, are growing right along with them.

It was through my understanding that God loves and cares so much for me that I was able, at last, to be close to my mother. After she and my father were divorced she had met and married a man she deeply loved. When he died a few years later she had gone to Alaska to visit friends, liked it there and stayed. Then she married again and I hadn't seen her in years.

Dottie, who had always been very close to Mom, went to Alaska too, married and stayed there. I had long been jealous of my sister's close relationship with our mother, and that probably had something to do with the fact that I seldom wrote to Mom, or took the time to call her. After the Gothard Seminar I saw how wrong and petty I had been, and I wanted to see my mother again, and to let her know that I was sorry and that I really loved her.

In March, 1981, she accepted an urgent invitation from Norm and me and came to visit us. She spent a week in our North Platte home and, for the first time, we seemed really to get acquainted with each other and to be aware of a closeness we, or at least I, hadn't known existed. I found that my mother, relieved of all the work and responsibility that had occupied her during my growing up years, was a fun-loving person and we had such a wonderful time that I could hardly bear to see her leave at the end of our week.

Norm and Mom took to each other in a big way and he began talking to her about coming to North Platte to live, now that she and her husband were retired. After she went home he said to me, "Honey, I'm so glad your mother came to see us and share her love with us. She's quite a lady, that mother of yours."

After Mom had gone I thought over every day and every hour of her visit and, in my new awareness of love and all that it means, realized how much I had missed, over the years, sharing in her tender, loving care. I knew I was the one who had cut myself off from her, but, even while she was here and we were getting to know each other so well, I still wasn't able to tell her all that was in my heart.

It has never been easy for me to express my love in words

and, even though I wanted terribly to tell Mom how much I really cared for her, I couldn't. So many times I wanted to say it right out, "Mother, I love you," but I didn't. Before she left I wished I could say to her, "Each day you were here it was a joy to say 'Good morning, Mother,' or to ask you a question and say 'Mother' each time before I asked it. But I didn't tell her.

The things we did together, shopping, eating out, just *being* together, had been so much fun. I had been so proud of her, so proud to introduce her to our friends; for she was still so beautiful, so regal, such a lovely lady, and our friends had had special and complimentary things to say about her. And when I chuckled again and again, recalling some of the funny things we'd done while she was with me, I realized that I had her to thank for my own sense of humor. It had come to me from her, and I knew then what a gift it is to be able to laugh and make others happy.

More than ever I was sorry that I had been so thoughtless over the years. I remembered all the times her phone should have rung or the mailman should have delivered a letter at her door, and didn't because I hadn't written the letter or made the call. And it was after her visit that I began truly to appreciate the wholeness and completeness of my present life, to know how blessed I was in having such a loving husband and mother, and it was a joy to be able to thank the Lord for giving them to me.

Naturally, I was overjoyed when, soon after returning to Alaska, Mother called to tell us that she and her husband were coming to North Platte to live. They made the move the following November, and now I have her near me, where I can see her every day and have her in my home, and go to hers. And now I can sympathize with Dottie, still far away in Alaska. She is the lonely one now, and I can understand and feel sorry for her in a way I couldn't have only a few years back. Once I would have thought "It serves her right." Now I can be happy for her when she and Mom (as happened last summer) can meet in Salt Lake and spend a few days together.

Chapter Sixteen

You Can't Go Home Again

In 1970 Norm took me back to Bingham Canyon. We were taking a vacation trip and I told him I'd like to see the old town again. I was sorry I went. The town had been fading when I moved away, nearly twenty years before; as the mine had been encroaching on it even then, buying up property at the top of the street, razing the buildings and chewing away at the ore underneath them.

On my last visit to my childhood home there had still been a good many buildings on either side of the narrow street. Now there was nothing left. I could hardly believe it. To me, Bingham Canyon had seemed to be a big place. How could it all have disappeared so completely?

The explanation lay in the growth and expansion of the copper mine. The St. Louis *Sunday Post-Dispatch* for November 21, 1971, tells it best in an obituary by George McCue. Under the headline, "The Open Pit Mine Becomes a Grave for Bingham Canyon, Utah," he wrote, "The city of Bingham Canyon died this month at the age of 103 following a lingering illness of more than a decade. The immediate cause of death was a

119

self-inflicted coup-de-grace: The few remaining residents of this once bustling mining community of 10,000 inhabitants went to the polls and voted to dissolve the municipal corporation. The tally was 11-2.

"The end was almost anticlimactic. The town had been in a slow decline since the late 1950s when Kennecott Copper Co. made it known that it was interested in extracting the estimated 3,000,000 tons of copper that lies deep beneath the main street in the town. Kennecott is the operator of the world's largest open pit mine, situated at the head of the canyon, just beyond the city limits. The pit is growing ever wider and deeper and was beginning to encroach on the town."

The company had finally coaxed and cajolled all but three of the property owners to sell. One of these had been the Federal Government "which [finally] accepted Kennecott's offer for the dignified brick and limestone neo-classical post office and built a new one (brick motel modern) further down the canyon."

"In the end the company went to court against [the last] two holdouts: the operator of a souvenir shop offering copper trinkets to tourists, and the town itself." The case never came to trial, however, for "in late December [1970] both the town and the souvenir shop owner agreed to accept a new company offer and the case was settled on the courthouse steps.

"In a few years the city of Bingham Canyon will be nothing but a memory floating in the air over the world's largest man-made hole, a cavity even today so vast that it confounds the imagination of the viewer. Tourists come at the rate of 200,000 a year and drive up the steep, dusty narrow road leading up the canyon to the parking lot and lookout station half way up the wall of the great pit. They push a button and a recorded deep male Voice of Kennecott intones the statistics: The pit is two and a half miles wide and a half mile deep. . . . If the hole were an amphitheatre, which, because of its terraced sides, it closely resembles, it would seat 9,000,000 spectators. From its flanks are extracted annually one half a billion pounds of copper, representing nearly a quarter of the entire United States production and nearly 10 percent of the known annual production of the world. The voice makes no mention of the city of Bingham Canyon."

How sad. A whole thriving, busy, happy town only a vanishing memory. The old Knight Hotel had disappeared into the great pit, as had Big Helen's place and Nick the Greek's. Even the enormous Bingham Merc was gone, every brick, board and nail, and the Evans Brothers' drug stores where I had played the big shot for such a little while. It didn't seem possible that the whole long, narrow street of happy memories could have become nothing but a great void where it was difficult even to picture the people and places I had once known so well.

I went into the souvenir shop and looked at the copper jewelry and artifacts they made and sold there, and finally made the last purchase I would ever make on the site where once had stood the city of my childhood. My souvenir was a little packet made up of a tiny copper hammer, screw driver and pliers.

Before I got in the car again, to leave Bingham Canyon behind forever, I stood a long time looking out over what was left of the canyon—and looking back on the all too few years I had spent there. Once more I saw us playing on the old railway trestles and the old tramway; sleigh riding on the steep street that was barely wide enough for two cars to pass. The old Knight Hotel was there in the shadows, the big lobby where I had loved to sit and visit with my friends, the miners who lived there, and watch them spit tobacco juice into the big spittoons. None of them ever used the spittoon nearest his chair but always aimed at the one on the far side of the big room—and hit it squarely every time. Their accuracy was amazing and fascinating.

With tears in my eyes I got into the car and we drove away. Until then I had not appreciated the privilege that had been mine in growing up in Bingham Canyon, where everyone had been friendly and happy. On summer evenings people sat on their steps, or the porches of their houses, all right up against the sidewalks, and anyone going by, kids and all, stopped to visit awhile. If the householders were eating or drinking anything, they shared. I knew everybody, all up and down the street and I remember them as warm, loving people, no matter what their race, religion or nationality.

I knew that I was not alone in such recollections, for over the years I had read several magazine articles and little books, written by one-time residents of Bingham Canyon: Dr. Richards, Dr. Frazier and Helen Zeese Papanikolas among them; and they all recalled the friendliness of the people, their kindness and happy regard for each other and especially for the town's small fry. Everybody looked out for us kids in one way or another. If anyone was stern with us it was for our own good—to protect us or to teach us needed lessons in obedience and regard for law and order and the welfare of others.

Chapter Seventeen

Keep On Keeping On

While I had been hospitalized at the time of my nervous breakdown, one of my roommates was a lady in her nineties. She was very ill and one or another of her three daughters was with her all of the time. One of the daughters, Nellie Yost, was a member of Riverside Church. I had met her there but knew her only slightly. We became better acquainted at the hospital, but it was not until later that I learned that she was an author who had written and published several books, mostly biographies.

Since my visit to Bingham Canyon I had thought a great deal about my childhood in that unusual town, and since my experience at the Gothard Seminar I had been wishing that I could write it all down, and maybe help someone else who needed help and guidance as I had in those dark, uncertain days of my self-doubt and resistance to the Lord's leading. Perhaps those two parts of my life would also make a book.

I knew that I could never write it myself—my spelling and grammar were too awful—but maybe Nellie Yost—.

Just before Christmas of 1981 I told her I had a story I

wanted to write, and asked her if she would advise me as to how to go about it. She invited me to come and talk it over. Shortly after the first of the year we met at her home and I told her some of my life story.

"Betty," she said at the end of our visit, "go home and write down everything you can remember about Bingham Canyon and about these last years. Then bring it back to me and we'll see what we have."

I was elated and excited. Nellie had been writing for thirty-five years. She had nine books in print and a new one coming out in a few months. Even though she was a tiny person I had looked up to her ever since I'd found out who she was and it had taken a lot of courage for me even to speak to her about my story. But I hurried home and did what she told me to, as best I could, and a few days later we met again. She read my notes, we talked some more, and then she said, "Betty, I'd like to write your story."

We went to work immediately. My writing is as impulsive and hurried as everything else I do. Nellie laughed about it, the way I'd left out words, even parts of sentences. Then she went ahead and dug the whole story out of me, all the details, the descriptions, everything she needed to tell it like it was.

I was amazed as I read each finished chapter; it was so exactly right, just the way I'd felt while experiencing all the things that had happened to me. It was as if they had happened to *her*, and when I asked her how she could do it, she told me she had learned to do that with each of her books, to put herself into the time and place of the person whose story she was telling, and to see and feel what they had seen and felt.

It has taken determination and perseverance, far more than we ever dreamed, to get this story on paper; for there have been many obstacles and delays. Illness, both hers and mine, set us back many weeks. I was able to help her while she was hospitalized and after she came home, and when my turn came and I had to have major surgery all the good Riverside people rallied round.

Norm and I had built a new house and moved in before it was quite all finished inside. There was still a good deal to do when I had to go to the hospital, and I'll never forget the wonderful surprise awaiting me when Norm helped me into the house the day I came home. All the varnishing and painting had been finished and the rooms, windows, floors and all were spick and span and shining clean. Richard and Gayle Anderson, Riverside friends, had done all that.

And then came the others, Lila Shimmin and Sandy Shimmin, Paula Dishman, Sandy Sale, Ruby Kittle and others, bringing home cooked meals for days. Norm was taking good care of me in every other way, but he *cannot* cook. If it hadn't been for those wonderful church friends we would have had to get along on carry-in meals from restaurants.

The cheerful visits of those good friends meant so much, too, in helping me get through the difficult days, but it was Lila, with her always confident advice to "keep on keeping on" that helped me most.

Of course work on the book had almost come to a standstill. Nellie, as usual, had to be out of town a great deal during the summer and my recovery was not coming along as well as we'd hoped. Spiritually I was fine, "keeping on" in good shape, but physically I wasn't doing too well. Dr. Ziegler was afraid more surgery would be necessary and I dreaded that.

I was still under the doctor's care and spending a part of every day in bed when Mom developed an acute heart problem. I was far from well but she was very, very ill. I had promised God, after Mom's visit to North Platte, that if He'd make it possible for her to come here to live and be near me I would be faithful in caring for her and making up to her for my long years of neglect.

Even though I was weak and in pain much of the time I prayed for the strength to care for her as long as she needed me. After many long frightening days, Mom began to get better and I was able to move her from the hospital to my home and look after her. In time my mother, though still frail, was fairly well again and, to my surprise, when I had time to think about it, so was I.

That autumn Nellie and I went back to work on my story.

Except in a spiritual way, I haven't changed much over the years since I first began visiting all up and down Bingham

Canyon's Main street. I still take several baths a day, I still love parades and celebrations, and my eye-doctor told me the other day that if I sit on my glasses one more time he doesn't think they'll take it.

I still manage to pull a bonehead caper every now and then, and each one seems to top the last. During my first hospitalization I had gotten to know many of the nurses and employees well. I liked them and usually looked some of them up whenever I went to the hospital to visit a friend. One day I learned that they badly needed some extra help. I was feeling pretty good then, and had the time, so I hired on as a tray line girl in the kitchen.

One of the first jobs assigned me was to take the big noon tray cart to the second floor where I worked. I was supposed to get on the elevator with the cart on the first floor, ride up to the second, get off with it and help distribute the trays. Simple enough, of course, for almost anyone but me.

Ever since my first elevator ride, years ago, I have been deathly afraid of the things. I don't know why, but for some reason being shut up in that tiny, windowless room terrorizes me. Many a time I have climbed umpteen flights of stairs to keep from riding on an elevator in stores, office and apartment house buildings.

I knew I wasn't going to ride that hospital elevator either, the first day I picked up my tray cart and wheeled it down to the door. So I pushed it into the cage, pushed the second floor button, backed out and ran like crazy to the stairway and up the steps and back to the elevator. I made it just as the door opened. I'd won the race—but I didn't feel too good about it.

I gave the matter a lot of thought that evening. I knew that elevator wasn't very dependable. It was very apt to skip a floor and go on to the next, and even down again to its starting point, before stopping where it was supposed to. I'd been lucky that first time, but chances were 50–50 that I couldn't do it again, and I *could* play tag with my cart until the food was all cold and the patients hollering for their trays. And if my superiors found out what was going on I'd very likely lose my job.

Even worse, I knew that what I'd done was dishonest. Among other duties, I was being paid to ride in the elevator with that tray cart and see that it arrived promptly where it was supposed to be. Therefore, I was *cheating* on my job and that bothered me. So I gave myself a good talking to, offered up a heartfelt prayer for strength and courage—and thereafter *rode* the elevator instead of racing it to the second floor. But that was only while chaperoning that cart. I still take the stairs at all other times.

My next big moment came during a spell of extremely cold weather. I was on my way home from town when I remembered that I had some letters in my handbag that had to be mailed that day. Pulling up to a curbside mailbox, I fished the letters out of my bag, then found that I hadn't parked close enough to reach the box from the car. From force of habit I pulled the key out of the ignition as I got out of my car to mail the letters. I still had it in my hand with the letters when I pulled the mailbox lid down and dropped them in, key and all.

My heart thunked down into my overboots when I saw what I had done. I looked at the mail pickup schedule on the box, and then at my watch. It would be over two hours, almost night, before the mailman would be along to collect the mail. Norm was at work and I wasn't about to call him to come to my rescue. Anyway I was in a strange neighborhood and I shrank from going to any of the houses to ask to use the telephone.

I just got back into my car and sat there in the freezing cold until the mailman drove up in his red, white and blue car to unload the box. Through chattering teeth I explained that I had mailed my key with some letters and asked him to please give it back to me. He laughed and said, "Honey, don't feel bad. You can't imagine what all people mail nowadays."

By 1982 times were getting tough in North Platte as well as everywhere else. Several members of our church had lost their jobs, business was suffering and Riverside Church was having a difficult time keeping up with expenses. Norm and I were having our troubles, too. We had invested quite a lot of money in some houses we had remodeled, or built from the ground up, and there was no sale for the properties. Norm was very good at carpentering, too, and during the past few years we had built or remodeled several really fine homes, sold them at a good profit and made quite a little money. But now we were in trouble. Taxes and interest were counting up and matters looked pretty bleak.

If it hadn't been for our faith in God, I'm sure I would have gone under again; but I had learned a lot since my former breakdown and now, along with Norm, I looked for the silver linings in the dark clouds; for I knew they were there if I'd take time to look. I found one of them the day I realized another of my dearest dreams.

As far back as I can remember I had wanted to be a singer—but the nearest I had ever came to it was back in my kid days when I danced and sang on the stage of the old *Princess* until Mr. Chesler chased me off. Of course I sang lustily in school with the rest of the kids, but the teachers never called on me for any solos or other special parts; it seemed there were always others better able to do those. As I grew older I realized that I really hadn't the voice, nor the ability, to be a successful singer, though I still longed to be one—but the real reason why I knew it could never be was that the very thought of getting up in front of *people* and singing turned me stiff with fright.

So the years went by and the only singing I did was in church, when the whole congregation was singing and no one could distinguish my voice from the others. I had been asked, of course. A time or two, when the Riverside choir had needed more voices, I had been invited to help out but had refused. I knew I didn't dare face the congregation and try to sing.

Then, about a year ago, with Old Fashioned Sunday coming up, I was again asked to sing. Old Fashioned Sunday is an annual fall event at Riverside, and practically the whole church takes part in the afternoon program that follows the noon picnic and barbecue. This time Donna Beardsley, one of my best friends, asked me to sing a duet with her, for our contribution. "Oh my, NO," I said. "I've never sung in public and I wouldn't dare." It didn't help any when she said, "I never have either, but I believe we can do it. God will help us."

I still refused—until Norm said, "Betty, you are being selfish. Where is your faith? Tell Donna you'll do it and you'll get along fine." We selected a hymn and practiced and practiced. I even began to feel a little confidence in myself. So the big day came, and then the hour. Others did their parts, some amusing, some sacred, but with every passing moment my confidence was oozing away and my stomach was beginning to churn.

Then, as we stood up to go up on the platform I whispered to Pastor Sell,* "Pray for me. Pray that I don't throw up before we're through." I was saying some prayers for myself, too; and then the piano part began. I opened my mouth on the right note—but not a sound came. It was only Donna who sang the first line. On the second line I managed a sound and joined in. We finished the hymn and the applause was satisfactory, but my legs were trembling so that I was afraid I'd not make it down the steps—and then Donna whispered, "Believe me, I was glad when you decided to join me on the second line." And then I realized that I had actually sung before an audience. Right there I thanked God that a little of my dream had finally come true.

Soon after that we had a "Singspiration" evening at Riverside, with members of some of the neighboring Independent Baptist Churches coming in to join us. Donna and I sang a number or two for that program, too, and since then have sung together several times. Who knows, I may yet realize my dream; for it's getting easier all the time.

---

*Daryl E. Sell.

Chapter Eighteen

Conclusion

My little family of the Bingham Canyon years really scattered as time went by. I had my mother near me now, but Dottie was still in Alaska and Dad in Salt Lake. Don, the kind and understanding brother who had counseled and looked after Dottie and me until he went into the service in World War II, had gone into government service, married and made his headquarters in Arizona. I seldom saw him after that and we didn't even keep in touch for a long time. His work kept him on the road a lot and I was busy raising my own family and living my own life.

With me stabilized in North Platte now, and Don finally retired in Arizona, we began calling each other at least once a month and having good visits by telephone. Then, a few weeks ago, Don called me from Salt Lake. He was living there now, he said, visiting his three children, but he wanted Mom and me to know that he wasn't well. He'd actually been sick for quite awhile and was feeling worse, he said.

Mom and I talked it over and decided to go to Salt Lake right away and see him. I was excited. I hadn't seen Don in fifteen years, and there were a lot of other family members I'd be glad to see: two of Mom's sisters, my dad and Sue and Shar, as well as several cousins, an uncle and Don's three children. Mom was excited, too, and I said we'd drive, so we'd have the car while we were out there. The thing was that I'd never driven more than fifty miles from home by myself—and Salt Lake was a twelve-hour drive to the west of us.

Norm couldn't get away from his job just then, and he was a little nervous at the idea of me driving all that way, and in Salt Lake, too. But I was sure I'd make it—and we didn't want to wait. Don had sounded pretty sick. Anyway, I'd prayed about it and felt that God would be with me.

When I started packing I decided I needed a new night-gown, so went downtown to get one. I hadn't bought a gown in quite a long while and was amazed at the prices marked on the tags, $15, $20, just for a flimsy little summer nightie. Finally I went into Woolworths, where, to my joy I found a table of sale merchandise and a gown in the lot for only $3. It was sealed up in a plastic bag but it was marked "medium" (my size), so I bought it and hurried home to finish packing.

I also decided to take along a little ice chest full of fudgecicles for snacks along the way, and a quart thermos bottle of coffee. We planned to leave at four-thirty in the morning, for I wanted to get into Salt Lake while it was still light. Mom came over to my house and I poured us each a half-cup of coffee and screwed the stopper back in the bottle. We drank the coffee, put our bags, the ice chest and the thermos in the car and headed out.

After awhile I told Mom that I was ready for a fudgecicle. She got the chest and opened it—and all we had in it was a pool of dark colored soup. Whatever it was, I'd done something wrong and every one had melted. "All right, then," I told Mom, "let's have a cup of coffee." She fished the thermos out of the back seat—and it was empty. I'd screwed the stopper in crooked and all the coffee had leaked out on the upholstery.

Otherwise the trip went very well and at five that afternoon we were in Salt Lake. Of course the town had grown and changed a lot since I'd been there and I no longer knew my way around. Mom, though, had been there several times since I had and she said we should take a certain road off the Interstate, but I was sure we should take a different one, so we did—and were lost for awhile. But it was still daylight when we found the motel where we were planning to stay, so the trip ended well.

We had decided it was best that we stay at the motel and then visit around among all the relatives, so we checked in and then called Don. He came to the motel for us, then took us to a restaurant for dinner. It was a very nice place and, after the hostess had seated us, I looked at Don and Mom; and then it hit me! For the first time since I was a kid the *three of us* were sitting down to dinner together. Mom and Don looked so happy and I said, "Oh, Mom, we are having a family *reunion*. You, Don and me." It was almost more than I could stand. I was so happy.

I'll always be thankful that we went to see my brother. He was so terribly thin and looked so ill, though he was still able to be up and about and to drive his car. A new treatment was helping him some, he said, and he was so glad to have us there.

After dinner we went back to our motel. We were all very tired and Don soon said goodnight and went to his daughter's. My new nightgown was still in its little plastic bag, so now I undressed and ripped the package open and held up my bargain to have a look at it. "Oh, Mom," I squealed, and held the garment up for her to see—and then we both laughed like idiots. I had bought a *child's* "medium" size gown. It wouldn't have covered *me* to my navel. No wonder it had cost only $3.00.

There was a big mall nearby, where it was cool and shady, with benches to rest on, and we spent a good deal of time there. Don and I would walk, arm in arm, then sit and rest awhile, and all the time we were talking and visiting. I told him that my friend and I were writing the story of my life and he was excited about that, too. I asked him if he remembered giving my ring to his girlfriend when they got engaged, and he laughed, and then asked me if I remembered giving *his* high school class ring to *my* boy friend—who wouldn't give it back when I asked for it. I had forgotten that.

We kept on remembering, and reminding each other of long forgotten things. I asked if he remembered when we lived at the hotel, while Grandma Lennon was still there, and she had tried to teach me to speak Italian. I was three or four then, and had soon balked. "Grandma," I told her, "Don't say those funny sounding words to me. *Talk like I know what you mean.*"

He didn't remember Grandma's satchel full of silver dollars, either. But that happened after Grandma moved to Salt Lake and, since Don usually went to visit our other grandmother on the farm, I was the one who went to Grandma Lennon's and the silver dollars were my memory. I was probably six or seven then, and when I visited I would insist on cleaning house for her. She always let me do whatever I pleased, and on one of my house cleaning stints I was straightening up her bedroom closet when I found the money.

It was in an old leather satchel with a flat bottom and a handle on top where it snapped shut. It was so full of silver dollars that I could hardly lift it off the floor. I don't know why she kept the coins there, or whether or not she ever spent any of them. Anyway, it was always full and I loved to lift the dollars in my hands and let them fall back into the satchel in a shining stream, and Grandma never minded me playing with her money.

Mom had a lot of time alone with Don, too, and for the rest of the five days we were there we gathered at the home of Don's daughter, Connie, or at my Sue's. Mom's sisters, and her brother Shirl and his wife were with us, and Don's other two children, and it did me good to see how lovingly they cared for him. I knew he was in good hands.

We had so much fun, remembering long ago happenings, and it seemed that most of the really weird things had happened to me. Like when Sue said, "Oh Mom, do you remember the time you let your pants go down the drain at the Tastee Treat?" That one really broke us up when she told it. I'd been washing out my underwear in a basin in the back room of the restaurant. There wasn't any sink there, just a drain hole, without a cover on it, in the floor. When I emptied the basin of dirty water into the hole I saw a pair of my panty briefs going down the hole with the water. I grabbed for them but was too late, they disappeared into the hole.

"Oh, well, they're gone," I thought, and forgot about it. The funny part came two or three days later when the toilet in the

133

men's room plugged up. We had to call a plumber, and Norm and I both stood watching him while he probed with his long hook into the toilet drain pipe. "Oh, oh, I've got it," he said, and pulled my pale pink lost panties up on the hook and waved them at Norm. His face had turned beet red, and I wanted to sink through the floor. Of all the places for those dratted pants to show up.

Then one of the girls asked me if I remembered the time Norm had to bale me out at the J. M. McDonald store in North Platte. I had forgotten that one, too. I guess our subconscious minds try to forget the most embarrassing things that happen, but Sue wasn't about to let *me* forget that one, either. After we gave up the Tastee Treat and Norm went to work on the railroad, I'd gotten tired of staying home and had hired on as a clerk at McDonalds. Of course I rated the store's employee's discount on anything I bought there and I had opened an account and become a very good customer. It was the Bingham Merc deal all over again—it was so easy to find things I liked and say "charge it." Of course I paid on the account out of every pay check, but the total just got bigger and bigger.

Finally I tired of working there. I wasn't feeling very well (it was the beginning of the nervous breakdown I had a little later) and I didn't like keeping to the work schedule any more. I resigned, and on the day I was to get my final check Norm took me to the store to pick it up—and that was when I found that what the store owed me didn't anywhere near equal what I owed the store. My good husband had to write a sizable check to bale me out, that time, else I'd have had to go back to work.

On our last day in Salt Lake Mom and I drove to a restaurant where we met Don and Aunt Ruby (the one whose courtship I had supervised at the old Knight Hotel so long ago) and had dinner. I'll never forget that evening, the family fun and memories, and all the laughing. Afterward Don took Mom to the motel and I drove back alone in my car. I could hear a queer noise in the engine, and thought it was probably the last fill of gas that was making it ping that way. But back at the motel I couldn't get the funny sound out of my mind. I didn't want anything to interfere with our last evening with Don, but finally I said, "Don, there's a funny sound in my engine. Will you listen to it?"

He did, and told me it wasn't the gas and that I'd better have a mechanic take a look. The Lord was really with me, for our motel was right next to an all night garage and when I had the mechanic look under the hood, he said, "Lady, you're lucky you came in. The bolts that hold the fan on the shaft are just ready to fall off." He tightened them up—and I thanked the Lord that I hadn't let it go and started home. What if those bolts had come off and the fan had gone through the radiator out on the interstate on the way home?

It was late on that July summer night when we told Don goodbye at the door of our motel. We'd had such a wonderful time and it was hard to say it, "Goodbye Brother;" but Don was the kind of man who was never afraid to say "I love you," and he made it as easy as he could for us and told us he'd be praying for a safe trip home for us—and so we parted. And all the way home I thanked God for giving us that wonderful visit with my brother.

* * * * *

My church is the home of my soul, the altar of my devotions, the hearth of my faith, the center of my affections, and fore-taste of heaven.

Albert Henry Kleffman

The Herrick Family.